© Copyright 2023 - All

The content contained within this bo
duplicated or transmitted without direct written permission from the author or the publisher.

Under no circumstances will any blame or legal responsibility be held against the publisher, or author, for any damages, reparation, or monetary loss due to the information contained within this book, either directly or indirectly.

Legal Notice:

This book is copyright protected. It is only for personal use. You cannot amend, distribute, sell, use, quote or paraphrase any part, or the content within this book, without the consent of the author or publisher.

Disclaimer Notice:

Please note the information contained within this document is for educational and entertainment purposes only. All effort has been executed to present accurate, up to date, reliable, complete information. No warranties of any kind are declared or implied. Readers acknowledge that the author is not engaged in the rendering of legal, financial, medical or professional advice. The content within this book has been derived from various sources. Please consult a licensed professional before attempting any techniques outlined in this book.

By reading this document, the reader agrees that under no circumstances is the author responsible for any losses, direct or indirect, that are incurred as a result of the use of the information contained within this document, including, but not limited to, errors, omissions, or inaccuracies.

Jimmy Carter: 99 Remarkable Tales From 99 Extraordinary Years

A Lifetime of Lessons and Stories

Anthony Dobbs

Table of Contents

INTRODUCTION 1

CHAPTER 1: EARLY LIFE 3
    1: Life in Archery 3
    2: An Early Understanding of Racial Prejudices—Winds of Change 4
    3: From Selling Salted Peanuts to Peanut Farming 6
    4: Friendships and Fun on the Farm 6
    5: School Life 8
    6: FFA Member 9
    7: Peewee 9

CHAPTER 2: NAVAL CAREER 11
    8: Difficulties in Admission to Naval School 11
    9: Life at Annapolis 12
    10: Marriage to Rosalynn Smith 13
    11: Family Life 14
    12: Submarine Duty 15
    13: U.S.S. *K-1* 16
    14: Rickover's Navy 16

CHAPTER 3: PEANUT FARMER TO PRESIDENT 19
    15: Hard Times 19
    16: End of Segregation Laws and the Carter Campaign 20
    17: State Senator 21
    18: Governorship on the Second Attempt 23
    19: "My Name Is Jimmy Carter" 24
    20: The Peanut Brigade, a Few Gaffes, and Victory 25
    21: President Jimmy 26

CHAPTER 4: LEADING WITH COMPASSION 29
    22: Amnesty to Draft Evaders 29
    23: A Man of the Masses 30
    24: Women's and Racial Empowerment 31
    25: Deregulation of Airline and Home-Brewing Industries 31
    26: The Energy Crisis 32
    27: Education and Health 33

CHAPTER 5: CARTER THE PEACEMAKER 35

28: CAMP DAVID—THE IDEAL PLACE TO FORGE PEACE 35
29: THE THREE MEN—DIVERSE YET UNITED IN PURPOSE 36
30: THE TALKS 37
31: THE ACCORDS—PEACE AT LAST 38
32: THE AFTERMATH—NOT ALL ROSY 39

CHAPTER 6: OTHER DIPLOMATIC SUCCESSES 41

33: THE PANAMA CANAL TREATIES 41
34: SALT 42
35: THE OLYMPIC BOYCOTT AND EMBARGOES ON THE SOVIET UNION 43
36: CHINA 44
37: AFRICA 44
38: SOUTH KOREA 45
39: CARTER DOCTRINE 45
40: NICARAGUA 46

CHAPTER 7: SURMOUNTING CHALLENGES 49

41: UGANDA AND IDI AMIN 49
42: DEPLOYMENT OF THE NEUTRON BOMB 50
43: THE CHRYSLER QUESTION 50
44: THE ROYAL CROWN OF HUNGARY 51
45: ALASKA 52
46: NATIVE AMERICAN SETTLEMENTS IN MAINE 52
47: THE COMMEMORATION OF DYLAN THOMAS 53
48: B-1 BOMBERS 54
49: CABINET REORGANIZATION 54

CHAPTER 8: LESSONS FROM DEFEAT 57

50: MISSED RHODES SCHOLARSHIP 57
51: GIVING UP THE NAVAL CAREER 58
52: RUNNING FOR GOVERNORSHIP 59
53: LOSS OF FAITH AND THE GAIN OF IT 60
54: CUBA 61
55: WOMEN'S RIGHTS 61
56: WANING POPULARITY—"MUSH FROM THE WIMP" 62
57: THE KILLER BUNNY EPISODE 63
58: THE IRAN HOSTAGE CRISIS 64
59: THE 1980 ELECTIONS 65

CHAPTER 9: HUMANITARIAN EFFORTS 67

60: THE CARTER CENTER 67
61: CONFLICT RESOLUTION IN NORTH KOREA 68

 62: Haiti 68
 63: The Fight Against Guinea Worm 69
 64: Building Homes for the Poor 70
 65: Emory University 71
 66: Mental Health Awareness Campaign 72

CHAPTER 10: PUBLIC SERVICE AND CIVIC ENGAGEMENT 73
 67: Author 73
 68: Sunday School 74
 69: Agriculture 75
 70: Carter Presidential Library and Museum 76

CHAPTER 11: FAMILY AND LEGACY 77
 71: Mama 77
 72: Daddy 78
 73: Rosalynn 79
 74: Gloria 80
 75: Ruth 81
 76: Billy 82
 77: Amy 83

CHAPTER 12: FRIENDSHIP, ALLIANCES, AND INFLUENCES 85
 78: A.D. 85
 79: Rembert 86
 80: Annie Mae 87
 81: Rachel Clark 87
 82: Julia Coleman 88
 83: Admiral Rickover 89

CHAPTER 13: FAITH AND OPTIMISM 91
 84: The Essay on Faith 91
 85: Inspiring Faith 92
 86: Spiritual Fitness 92
 87: Practicing What He Preached 93
 88: The Malaise Speech 94

CHAPTER 14: EMBRACING CHANGE AND EVOLUTION 97
 89: Rock N' Roll President 97
 90: Carpentry 98
 91: Writing and Poetry 99
 92: Winemaking 99
 93: Hunting and Fishing 100
 94: Painting 101
 95: Environmentalism 101

CHAPTER 15: A LIFE OF SERVICE AND PURPOSE 103
   96: "Don't Get Weary, Don't Be Afraid, Don't Give Up." 103
   97: "A Life Very Well Done" 104
   98: A Full Life 105
   99: Shining Ex-President 105

CONCLUSION: 99 AND COUNTING 107

ABOUT THE AUTHOR 111

REFERENCES 113

Introduction

There is an interesting anecdote about Jimmy Carter that he personally narrated to a gathering at Paramount Theater in Seattle, in 2012. Long ago, when he was fresh from the White House, he traveled to Osaka in Japan. He was the chief dignitary at a graduation ceremony in a small college there. He realized at the outset that it took longer to say what he was saying in Japanese. To make the job of the translator easy, he selected one of his shortest, but not funniest, jokes. He was a little surprised to notice that the translator seemed to use fewer words to interpret this joke to the audience. But there was no doubt that the latter seemed to enjoy it. Everyone doubled up in laughter, much to the President's pleasure. Later, after his speech, when he was in the green room, Carter asked the translator to tell him how he managed to convey the essence of the joke in so few words. The translator seemed ill at ease with the question, evading it and trying to change the subject. However, Carter was insistent, and finally, the translator replied that he just told everyone that President Carter had told a joke and that they must all laugh. Carter says humorously that incidents like these remind him of a cartoon he saw in *The New Yorker*, where a little boy, asked about what he wants to be when he grows up, quips with his answer—a "former President."

Stories like these remind us why Carter is so lovable even four decades after his presidency has ended. Carter today holds the title of being the longest-lived, oldest-living, and longest-married president, who has had the longest post-presidency term of 42 years. He is also the third oldest living former state leader in the world (*Is Jimmy Carter*, 2023).

If Carter was known as a peace-loving politician who was often derided for his "too-soft" policies in his day, he is remembered more now for his humanitarian activism after his presidency. For example, in 2002, he was awarded the Nobel Peace Prize. But perhaps, in crediting only

Carter as a humanitarian, we have long done a disservice to his persona and the strengths of his presidency.

In an interview with *The Guardian,* when asked about the greatest achievement of his time as President, Carter said without hesitation (Cadwalladr, 2011):

We didn't fire a single shot...didn't kill a single person....didn't lead [the] country into a war—legal or illegal. We kept our country at peace. We never went to war. We never dropped a bomb. We never fired a bullet. But still, we achieved our international goals. We brought peace to other people, including Egypt and Israel. We normalized relations with China, which had been nonexistent for 30-something years. We brought peace between the US and most of the countries in Latin America because of the Panama Canal Treaty. We formed a working relationship with the Soviet Union. (para. 40)

What greater glory can there be, especially in this mostly trigger-happy world of ours, than to say that he met all the burden of public expectations set upon him without once taking a life directly or indirectly as a leader? What greater testament can there be to his personality than to concede that he, who was at the helm of affairs for one of the most powerful nations in the world, refused to fall prey to the need to make a public display of his country's might in order to get things done?

Jimmy Carter: 99 Remarkable Tales From 99 Extraordinary Years hopes to retell the story of Jimmy Carter, a man of immense talent, who has worn so many hats, and achieved so much, but has stayed grounded to his roots, family, and values. It will look at important chapters from his life, from a childhood spent in Plains, Georgia, to the legacy he leaves for the world as he celebrated his 99th birthday in October 2023. What perhaps sets this book apart from its contemporaries is that herein we seek to celebrate Carter's life with a short incident or story for each year that he has lived—99 stories to commemorate the long, but truly purposeful life that Carter has carved out for himself, despite the odds.

Chapter 1:

Early Life

Jimmy Carter was born the eldest son of James Earl Carter and Bessy Lillian Carter née Gordy, in 1924. James Earl Carter was primarily a businessman and agriculturist who had a general store and farmlands in Plains, Georgia, while his wife, who was more popularly known by her middle name, Lillian, was a registered nurse in the nearby Wise Sanitarium hospital. Incidentally, Jimmy was the first US president to be born in a hospital.

For most of his childhood, Jimmy grew up on his father's farmland, often toiling away, and learning more about it. His parents, who had to raise the family in and around the Great Depression in the '30s, had to move the family several times. Thus, Jimmy grew up in places like Archery, which was home to many poor African-American families. This phase was also the beginning of many lifelong friendships that Jimmy would cherish with people of the Black community. It was also when Jimmy began to understand that the removal of segregation was long overdue. Much later, this would be one of the foremost causes that he would strongly support.

1: Life in Archery

It was when Jimmy turned around 4 years of age that his dad purchased their house in Archery. It was a regular, tan, "shotgun" style house with a hall that separated the three bedrooms on the right from the dining room, kitchen, and living rooms on the left side. A storehouse at the back of the house, separated by a screen door, was where extra water, corn for the chickens, and wood were kept. A front porch allowed the Carters to gather informally during the hotter months of the year.

Initially, this house had no electricity or piped water. In fact, they had to draw water in pails from the well to use in the kitchen. Waste was collected in slop buckets in bedrooms and then emptied into the outhouse behind the house. It was only in 1935 that Earl Carter bought a windmill with an overhead tank and established pipes so that the house could have a running water supply.

In the evenings, kerosene lamps were used for light and the household considered it sinful to burn them in a room not being used. This would mean that only those parts of the house where people were gathered were lit. Rural electrification came in 1938, and until then, the house had only two luxuries to speak of—a large Aladdin lamp for reading in the front room, and a battery-operated radio which kept them entertained and updated about world news, which they used sparingly. Once electricity came, the house was slowly updated with better amenities such as electric lighting, a fridge, and an electric stove.

The summers may have been hot, but the winters were even more excruciating. After waking up they had to start a fire either in the fireplace or one of the rooms to keep the house warm enough. This was hard work as the smaller and lighter pieces of wood had to be carried in and used to light the bigger logs.

A young Jimmy helped his father with all the chores in and around the house and farm. Even before he was of age to be engaged in the fields, he learned the operations of farming from the Black overseer, Jack Clark. He often followed Clark around like a puppy peppering him with questions about work on the farm. Jack Clark was one of Jimmy's earliest friends.

2: An Early Understanding of Racial Prejudices—Winds of Change

A young Jimmy knew vaguely that though they worked closely with the Blacks on the farm, they were not the same as them. His father, Earl, was, from the beginning, a staunch pro-segregationist, who believed that Whites and Blacks ought not to mingle socially. But Jimmy's mother, who was a nurse, believed that her mission was to serve everyone, no matter the color of their skin. She was much more progressive than the Whites of her time.

One of the most respected Black men of Archery, Bishop William Decker Johnson, was on good terms with the Carter family. Every year, he would invite the Carters to a special mass at St. Mark's African Methodist Episcopal (AME) Church, where the regular mass would be followed by the bishop's sermon. Jimmy, used to going to the Baptist Church in their community, was often amazed by the overflowing AME church, their peppy devotional songs, and their strong religious sentiments, which were in stark contrast with the rather subdued and shorter mass of his own church. During the sermon, he would also notice how the Bishop, who was well-read and a master in the English language, would often adopt the accent and speech of the hardly literate sharecroppers to better emphasize his messages.

Even though Bishop Johnson was respected by everyone in the community, he never approached the Carter household from the front door. When he wanted to visit them, he often came in his chauffeured Cadillac or Packard and honked outside the gate, where Jimmy's father would go and meet him. Jimmy often saw his father and the bishop talking and laughing together, though he never once saw his father inviting him in.

Years later, when Alvan Johnson, the bishop's son, would come to visit Jimmy's mother, he would come to the front door, be invited in, and be seated with his mother in the parlor or the porch. Since the people of the South were traditionally known for their hospitality, Jimmy supposed their father made peace with this. To his knowledge, he never heard his dad chastising his mother for inviting in a Black. But Jimmy also observed how Earl pointedly ignored these visits, almost as though they never happened.

These minor incidents would shape Jimmy's opposition to racial segregation later in life.

3: From Selling Salted Peanuts to Peanut Farming

As young as 5 years old, Jimmy became an entrepreneur. His job was to sell boiled peanuts around Plains. He used to take his wagon into the fields and gather the peanuts. Tugging home the wagon, he would clean the peanuts and soak them in salt water overnight. The next day, he would cook the peanuts in water for half an hour. After they dried thoroughly, Jimmy would pack them into paper bags and carry them around in a basket in the town and sell them. Later, he would cycle to the town and make about a dollar when all the sacks were sold.

Jimmy had regular customers who would readily buy from him, like Bud Walters, the cobbler. There were also extremely polite visitors who would either buy or decline. Finally, there were the town loafers who often mocked Jimmy for being unable to sell all his sacks.

Peanuts were, in fact, a great source of revenue for the Carter family, who had extensive farmlands of 360-odd acres. Their main stash crops were, like other farmers in the area, peanuts and cotton. When Jimmy was old enough, his father would make him work on the field after school hours and the entire day on Saturdays when there wasn't school. Harvest time saw every able-bodied man on the farm shaking the plants to clean the dirt off them, and then stacking them for drying.

Thus, Jimmy Carter's association with peanut farming and selling began as early as he could remember.

4: Friendships and Fun on the Farm

Jimmy's friends were the sons of Black sharecroppers who resided in clapboard houses around the farm. They had great fun swimming, fishing, working together, exploring, and playing around the vast lands that belonged to his father. As children, none of them had the time to ponder about the differences between them, and they had fun despite the fact that Jimmy hailed from the "big house."

However, the differences would slowly get bigger and more difficult to ignore. While Jimmy went to the local Plains High School, his friends would go to an all-Black school, which was usually held in private homes or church rooms filled to the brim with students of different ages and grades. The furniture and books used at these schools were usually hand-me-downs from the students at the White school. While it was mandatory for White boys to maintain a specific attendance at school, the Blacks were treated with more leniency, as it was understood that their services would be required by the lands that employed them. More than elementary education for a Black man was considered a luxury.

At the time, Jimmy's best friend was A.D., the son of a Black sharecropper. His other playmates included Rembert Forrest, the only other White kid in the group and the adopted son of a White farm and sawmill owner, and Edmund Hollis, who was A.D's cousin. Milton and Johnny Raven, two brothers who lived about half a mile away from the Carter farm, also occasionally joined.

Jimmy was given a pony, Lady, for Christmas shortly after he turned 7. A.D. and he often rode the stocky little creature around the farm. But Jimmy's father believed that everyone on the farm ought to contribute their share, even a pony. Thus, they had Lady mate with Rembert's stallion at proper intervals. Jimmy was always delighted with the birth of the colts. Eventually, however, each of them was sold away for $25 each by his father, a situation that saddened him. As he grew older, Jimmy tired of riding, and yet dreaded his father's taunt asking him when he had last ridden Lady. His father often compared the cost of the pony's upkeep—the food it ate vs. the hours of productive service it yielded as Jimmy's ride.

5: School Life

Jimmy started school when he was 6 years old, but it in no way reduced the centrality of his home and family in his heart. He woke up early, even on school days, to complete chores around the farm. For a long time, he was the one in charge of milking the cows. After his work, he would attend school, only to rush back from home to resume his work on the farm.

At school, most of his classmates hailed from poor families. Most of the children walked barefoot and had to tread carefully to avoid splinters. It was not until he was 13 that Jimmy started wearing shoes to school and church. As such, hookworm affliction was quite common because the parasite entered the human body through the feet when one walked on contaminated soil. The school was also a place where, in addition to knowledge, infections and diseases were exchanged and spread rapidly. Lice infestation was so common that if one of their classmates kept on their hats for the entire day, they instantly knew what the problem was. Additionally, other contagious diseases such as malaria, typhoid, and typhus spread by insects and rodents were also omnipresent. Students who contracted diseases such as polio were merely kept at home, while others feared that they would be the next ones to catch it. Being admitted to the hospital for serious illnesses was uncommon at the time.

For most of his life, Jimmy was about as shy and timid in the classroom as he was confident, loud, and outspoken on the farm. He was, however, good at studies and could read and write without any difficulty. He managed to keep his grades on par with the cleverest in the class. One of the things that helped Jimmy was his extensive reading. When not engaged in any work at the farm, you would find him with a book. Very soon, he was recognized as one of the best readers in his class, often winning contests for having read the greatest number of books.

Jimmy missed out on being the valedictorian owing to collective truancy from his class, of which he was a part. In senior year, he and a couple of other boys absented themselves from class and went to the town of Americus for a movie and a day out. They even inserted an article in the local newspaper about their exploits. When they returned, all of them were given a zero for every subject for a week, and seven licks each before being readmitted to the classroom.

6: FFA Member

One of the biggest advantages of attending school for Jimmy was becoming a member of the Future Farmers of America (FFA) initiative of the government. Via the organization, Jimmy learned about caring for farm animals, pest control, food processing, and subjects related to farming and herding. It also conducted workshops for carpentry, furniture making, metalworking, and welding. Carpentry and woodwork would go on to become one of Jimmy's lifelong passions.

FFA also conducted a series of competitions related to speaking, crafting, and other skills for a successful agriculturist. Jimmy was an FFA officer while at school and attended several national conventions being a part of it. He was also able to learn shorthand and typing through this organization, skills that greatly helped him as an author later. Jimmy was also able to use some of the knowledge he picked up at Future Farmer's class to make improvements on his farm, such as the A-frame hog-farrowing structures he helped his father build, which would help keep the animals dry, allowing for the convenient feeding of the babies, without being inadvertently crushed by the heavy sows.

7: Peewee

Jimmy was smaller than most boys of his age, but that did not prevent him from being an excellent basketball player who made the varsity team in the final years of school. He was nicknamed Peewee, after a comic cartoon character of the same name, who was known for his diminutive stature. Very soon, it became evident that Jimmy was also one of the fastest players on the team. This was a huge advantage when the team relied on fast passes when the ball was on the opposing team's side of the court.

The competitions were often held in other schools where the team traveled by bus. Most of these matches were held at night so that parents with day jobs could also attend and cheer on their kids. Apart from basketball, he also enjoyed playing tennis, and other games whenever he got the time for it.

Chapter 2:

Naval Career

Jimmy's wish was to join the Naval Academy like his maternal uncle, Tom Giordy. The latter used to send him letters and postcards from the beautiful ports that they were docked at, which fanned Jimmy's resolve all the more. Jimmy set his sights on Annapolis, Maryland, the seat of the U.S. Naval Academy. Even as he was in grade school, Jimmy composed a letter to the academy enquiring about how one could gain admission there. He would have to wait a bit, but eventually, he did enroll and complete his course.

8: Difficulties in Admission to Naval School

Jimmy realized that there were a couple of requirements to get selected into the Naval Academy. The first of the conditions was something that Jimmy worried least about. He knew grades wouldn't hinder him when he put in his application.

The other eligibility requirements were things he constantly worried about. The Navy would only take in candidates who met a certain height and weight requirement, for instance. Hard to believe it as it may be, the candidates had to have straight teeth—something Jimmy did not. The physical requirements were something that Jimmy worked on.

Most importantly, though, candidates had to have a letter of endorsement from the local senator or congressman. Jimmy's father actively widened his circle of friends and actively sought the support of Congressman Steven Pace during Jimmy's last year of school. But as luck would have it, Pace had already sent in his recommendation of another candidate for that year. As you can imagine, Jimmy was disappointed, but he still did not give up. That was also the year Japan attacked Pearl Harbor, and the US entered WWII. Jimmy was now certain that a naval career was exactly what he wanted. He even had it planned down to the minor details—he would become a submarine commander in the U.S. Navy!

As per Pace's suggestion, Jimmy took up subjects at junior college that would stand him in good stead as he applied for the post of midshipman. But even the next year, Pace did not appoint Jimmy. Earl Carter literally had to confront Pace for him to assure them that he would give Jimmy the letter the next year and that he would be exempted from some of the entrance exams should his grades at college be good enough.

Jimmy transferred out of junior college to Georgia Tech, an engineering college in Atlanta, which was thought to be more beneficial for his career prospects. After a year at Georgia Tech, as promised by Pace, Jimmy finally made it to Annapolis.

9: Life at Annapolis

It was not a bed of roses by any account. Jimmy had it hard at the academy. At almost 19, in June 1943, Jimmy took a train to Washington D.C., followed by a bus to the academy. He just about managed to pass the height and weight requirements necessary for his admission.

As on any campus, the freshers were ragged and called the "plebs" by the seniors. They were made to act, sing, or do push-ups. Noncompliance was met with stricter forms of punishment, such as being thrashed with brooms. In one of his diary entries, Jimmy wrote about how sore his bottom was after one such ordeal.

The academy's motto could have been written for a person like Jimmy: *Another week in which to excel!* Jimmy was self-disciplined and woke up early every day. A year later, Jimmy was on his first mission as a trainee onboard a ship. The practice session included aspects of ship operations and maintenance procedures, and handling guns to fire at enemy aircraft.

Apart from the rigors of his training, Jimmy continued to read about everything under the sun. He also developed a strong love for classical music from his roommate, who had a fine collection of records. He channeled his innate love for sports by becoming an enthusiastic cross-country runner. He also took an interest in naval aviation, whereby he learned to take off and land an aircraft on water.

After three years of studying at Annapolis, Jimmy graduated in 1946.

10: Marriage to Rosalynn Smith

Right after graduating from the Naval Academy, Jimmy married his sweetheart, Rosalynn Smith, a neighbor to the Carters and a good friend of Jimmy's youngest sister, Ruth. Unbeknownst to Jimmy, Ruth and Rosalynn had already made plans for him to marry her. But at the time, Jimmy had only been interested in dating girls closer to his own age.

Toward the end of his stint at Annapolis, when he came home, Ruth was dating a boy and they invited Jimmy to the movies with them. As they passed the Methodist Church they met Rosalynn, who also agreed to accompany them. The rest, as they say, was history. Rosalynn was swept off her feet, while Jimmy was suddenly aware that his sister's little friend was all grown up. They talked for a long time, and Jimmy found her to be beautiful, intelligent, shy, and yet uninhibited about her opinions.

The next morning, his mother asked him about what he had done the previous night. Jimmy said he went to the movies with Rosalynn Smith. He declared that she was the one he would marry.

When he returned to Annapolis, Jimmy and Rosalynn continued to write to each other. When he came home for a short break, he proposed to her. She initially said no, not because she did not want to be with him, but because she had vowed to her dying father that she would complete college. She eventually agreed to marry him in 1946 after meeting his parents and graduating from junior college at Georgia Southwestern College.

A funny incident from their marriage in Plains was that Jimmy, who was generally punctual to the minute, was late for his own wedding. This was because he had to pick up Rosalynn from her home on his way to the church, and he had not allotted enough time for that.

11: Family Life

Rosalynn and Jimmy moved to Norfolk, Virginia, close to where his ship was stationed. The new recruits to the Navy were given projects based on the draw of lots and Jimmy was stationed onboard one of the oldest battleships that was still being used, the U.S.S *Wyoming*. The ship had by then completed about 33 years of service, including being used during battle in WWI and for training during WWII.

His assignment kept Jimmy away for long hours, even on weekends, leaving Rosalynn to her own devices to keep herself entertained. She was quite lonely, being away from her friends and family for the first time in her life.

At this point, Jimmy was making only a meager $300 per month, which was just enough to cover their expenses. When Jimmy was home, they could not afford to eat out or go to the movies often. He bought a record player and listening to music records was one way in which the young couple bonded and had fun.

In 1947, the Carters welcomed their first son, John William Carter, fondly nicknamed "Jack." The next two sons were also born in quick succession in 1950 and '52—James Earl III called "Chip," and Donnel Jeffrey, nicknamed "Jeff." More than a decade later, in 1967, the couple would also go on to have their only daughter, Amy Lynn, when their eldest was 20.

If Rosalynn found single parenting and managing a house difficult on her own, she tried to get through the task smiling, because that is how her husband always dealt with situations.

12: Submarine Duty

In 1948, Jimmy had the option of selecting a specialization among intelligence operations, submarines, or naval air force. This was Jimmy's opportunity and he grabbed at it with both hands. He, Rosalynn, and Jack moved to Connecticut, where an intensive training camp was held for men who wanted to join submarine duty. Here, they were given training in the construction and operation of the submarines, the use of torpedoes, and the maintenance of the vessel and its parts.

After the completion of the six-month training, Jimmy was stationed on U.S.S. *Pomfret,* which was docked at Honolulu and would leave for China soon. It was during this cruise that a raging storm hit his vessel. Jimmy was seasick for most of this journey. He would borrow extra watch duties on the bridge of the vessel from other officers, simply to experience the fresh air above, rather than be in the claustrophobic rooms of the submarine below. He was swept off by a wave into the waters during such a watch. It was his first near-death experience. Luckily for him, when the wave receded, he was on the main deck and was able to cling to one of the five-inch guns there for support.

The storm was so fierce that communication with the *Pomfret* was lost. Word was sent out to the wives and families of the men who were in Hawaii that the vessel and its crew were deemed to be lost at sea. Rosalynn, who was in Georgia at the time, did not receive the heartbreaking news and, thus, remained unaware of the danger Jimmy was in. Three days later, the *Pomfret* was able to transmit news of their survival and continue the journey.

13: U.S.S. *K-1*

In 1950, officers on submarine duty were informed that the navy was building a new submarine based on snorkel air intake and new technology that would ensure its movement through water quieter than earlier vessels. The submarine was named *Killer-1* and called *K-1* for short. Enthusiastic as ever, Jimmy submitted his name and oversaw the final building and testing of the craft.

The project was exciting because of the latest features incorporated into the mission, and the possibility of conflict with the Soviets during the Cold War era. *K-1* was stationed around the Atlantic Caribbean region and was submerged for many days as part of its testing process.

Jimmy had to fight a fire that erupted in the engine room once while the vessel was fully submerged. It was imperative that any fire should be dealt with as quickly as possible due to the proximity of electrical equipment within a submarine. Similarly, the toxic fumes from a fire, if unchecked, could easily suffocate and kill the men within. As the engineering officer, Jimmy was the lead firefighter. He put on his protective gear and mask and extinguished the flames using carbon dioxide and dry powder. The last thing he remembered was speaking into his headphones to the captain that the fire was under control. When he woke up, he was on one of the messroom tables with a hospital man trying to make him breathe oxygen. Jimmy vomited for a while but was soon fine physically.

14: Rickover's Navy

A very confidential program of building submarines that would be propelled by nuclear power was being undertaken under Captain Hyman Rickover. He was personally recruiting promising submariners for the mission. Jimmy's application was met with an interview call with Rickover himself.

Captain Rickover had courted enough controversy to become somewhat of a celebrity within the naval ranks. He had repeatedly gone against naval procedures and regulations. Admirals voted against his promotion, and it was only President Truman's personal intervention that had kept him in service.

Jimmy was understandably nervous about this meeting and prepared well for the interview. It was a two-hour long discussion on subjects Jimmy named, and on which Rickover asked him a series of questions increasing in complexity until he was unable to answer any more. The subjects were both technical and general, such as naval history, submarine battle tactics, electronics, gunnery, books, and music. His last question to Jimmy was, "How did you stand in your class at the Naval Academy?" Jimmy answered proudly that he stood 59th in a class of 820. Rickover never complimented him but merely asked whether he had always done his best. Jimmy was on the verge of saying yes when he thought of all the missed opportunities, and replied, "No, sir, I didn't always do my best." Rickover only said, "Why not?" before swiveling his chair around and ignoring Jimmy, indicating the interview was over.

Jimmy thought the interview had gone poorly and conveyed the same to Rosalynn but was surprised to learn that he had been selected after all. It was probably his honesty in the last question that had earned him a place in Rickover's navy.

Chapter 3:

Peanut Farmer to President

In 1953, just as Jimmy was making advances in his career, he got the painful news that his father was battling pancreatic cancer and that the chances of recovery were negligible. He got permission from Rickover to be with his father for two weeks. In July 1953, Earl Carter passed away in his home in Plains. After the funeral, Jimmy decided to give up his naval career and take over his father's affairs. It had been over 12 years since Jimmy had moved away from Plains, and it was with trepidation that he looked forward to his homecoming. This was especially true because Rosalynn, who had always stood by him, was furious with him over this decision. As a navy man's wife, she had been taking care of their home with independence, and the return to their rural hometown was a move she could not comprehend. Since there was no longer an assured income for the family of five, they had to take up residence in one of the government's housing projects in Plains.

15: Hard Times

After so many years away from home, Jimmy was out of touch with the latest farming practices. It was the middle of the harvest season, and there was plenty of work to be done, in addition to which there were debts owed to his father that not all had paid up. The bigger problem was that there were pending taxes to be paid to the government. Much to Jimmy's surprise, he also ended up being the executor of his father's estate. He divided the estate into five equal holdings—one each for his mother and four siblings. After everyone had made their respective choices as to which portion of the holdings they wanted, Jimmy took the last piece of land for himself.

To Jimmy, the rigors of farming looked much more daunting than all the hardships he had borne in his naval career. He took crash courses and read up as much as he could about the plantation of corn, peanuts, and cotton. He also had to look after woodlands that yielded timber on the lands. But with time, he got better equipped to handle everything. His eldest was admitted to the same school that Jimmy and Rosalynn had attended. They attended the Baptist church, the one where Jimmy was baptized. He also used the spare time he got to make rudimentary furniture for the little home they now lived in.

Eventually, in a couple of years, with a couple of loans, the farmlands grew. Jimmy's brother Billy and his mother became minor partners in the farming business and the other affairs of the family business, including selling supplies to other farmers. Jimmy and Rosalynn held about 3,200 acres of farmland and their main crop was peanuts. Jimmy was also elected the president of the Georgia Crop Improvement Association, which specialized in the production and distribution of crops such as cotton, corn, wheat, and pinewood. For the next 23 years, the Carters continued in the business until Jimmy became the president.

16: End of Segregation Laws and the Carter Campaign

As his business grew, Rosalynn and Jimmy became more active in the community life of Plains. They were active church members and Jimmy frequently taught Bible lessons on Sundays. They went for country dances at a local club and played golf at the course in Dawson with friends. Jimmy also became a board member of the Sumter County Board of Education. Though segregation had ended a while ago, the schools in Plains, Georgia, continued with the old tradition. The schools for White children were infrastructural sound and well-maintained, while the Black schools were still held with children crammed into small classrooms. The Black children had no school buses, and when they were finally introduced, the fenders of the buses were painted black to remind everyone that these buses carried Black and not White students.

Jimmy used a program sponsored by Billy Graham to fight for a biracial faith community. Yet no church, Black or White, would permit such a program on their land. Eventually, the program was held at an abandoned school in Americus. A film on how Blacks and Whites could become equal participants in church and missionary work was screened. Hundreds of people belonging to both communities watched it side-by-side, a first-of-its-kind event in the conservative Plains community.

However, as the unrest over segregation became more widespread, Jimmy and Rosalynn's progressiveness was condemned. A delegation of the White Citizens Council requested Jimmy pay his annual membership fees, which he refused to do. Some of the customers the Carters catered to started avoiding them, and once, Jimmy was refused gasoline at a station. Even so, the Carters refused to bow down to societal pressure. They knew that it was high time that segregation ended and they decided to match their actions to their beliefs.

17: State Senator

Jimmy knew very little about politics, though his father had served in the state legislature and their family had always been staunch Democrats. When Jimmy felt the need to do more for Black–White integration in schools, he decided that he ought to try his hand at politics, so that he could personally spearhead and implement change.

On the day he decided to put in his name for the state senatorial candidacy at the courthouse, he was changing into a suit and tie when Rosalynn, unaware of his plans, asked him whether he was going to attend a funeral. When he told her of his plans, she was pleased. His opponent was Homer Moore, an honest warehouseman and peanut trader from Jimmy's mother's hometown. Each one of them had an advantage in their respective communities. The senate district catered to about 75,000 people from seven counties, and Jimmy had to win over their trust if he was to succeed.

On election day, a big problem in Georgetown almost upset Jimmy's dream. A local political boss, Joe Hurst, was tampering with the ballots and even discarding votes to help Moore against Jimmy. Jimmy immediately called a reporter he knew and asked him to record what was happening. Unfazed at being observed, Hurst continued to illegally cast aside votes that were not for Moore. In every other county, the election results were close between Moore and Jimmy. In Georgetown, though only 333 people had voted, the results were declared as 360–136 in favor of Moore, a clear case of election fraud.

Jimmy was so angry that he contested the result and made a petition for a recount. Very soon, the press got involved in the sensational case, with caricatures of the elections showing Hurst in a poor light doing the rounds. When the case came up before the judge, it became increasingly clear where the truth lay. The result of the Georgetown election was invalidated, which gave Jimmy an edge over Moore. Jimmy became the Democratic candidate without a Republican opponent.

His hurdles were far from over, though. Even up to the last day, he knew that his candidature could be contested again and that Atlanta may refuse to swear him in. Jimmy waited with bated breath and on the day, when his name was called, he was sworn in at last without any hitches as the senator.

As a senator, Jimmy worked at improving the electoral system first and foremost. His naivete was soon replaced by an understanding of how dirty politics could get and he vowed to clean up the system. Secondly, he was hell-bent on providing a four-year college in Southwest Georgia so that students would not have to travel far for higher education. This proved to be a difficult task, but Jimmy was a hard bargainer and, ultimately, the college was established. It is not difficult to see why he was re-elected for another term as the senator.

18: Governorship on the Second Attempt

The first time Jimmy ran for the governorship of Georgia, he had very little money or connections. He was disillusioned that a known segregationist, Lester Maddox, had been appointed. For a while, Jimmy was intensely bitter about the defeat and even lost his faith, until Ruth, his sister, who was by then an evangelist and author, advised him to learn lessons from his defeat, strengthen his religious faith, and prepare for alternative goals in life.

Jimmy concentrated on his business and missionary life for a while, until he rallied and decided to run for governorship a second time in 1970. At the time he announced his candidature formally at the Capitol, he carried a two-year-old Amy in his arms. This time, he did not use any billboards or public announcements. Instead, he met people, forged new connections, took courses to remember people and their names, and participated and spoke at public events so that people started recognizing him. It was a quiet, clever, and candid strategy for winning the trust of his people.

In one such event, Carter was meeting with the public and shaking hands with everybody. He proffered his hand to a young man who at first ignored him and then punched him in the jaw. It turned out that the man was an ex-marine who had been discharged from service owing to mental health problems.

Carl Sanders, Jimmy's opponent, had already served as governor from 1963–67. He was well-known, wealthy, and influential. Newspapers and popular endorsements ran his campaign slogan: "Carl Sanders ought to be governor again." Sanders' extravagant lifestyle was contrasted with Jimmy's humble farming background. Clearly, they hoped to dazzle the public with Sanders' money and social prestige. Moreover, Sanders' personal ties with the Blacks were often used to misconstrue Jimmy's more moderate support for the cause as "racism." Slowly but steadily, Carter made inroads into public awareness and hearts. In fact, Jimmy's chosen symbol was that of the peanut, which his supporters wore as their lapels and pendants. He finally won the governorship in 1970.

19: "My Name Is Jimmy Carter"

A term of being the governor imparted several valuable lessons to Jimmy. He learned to streamline governmental agencies, cutting them down to only the necessary ones where required. He worked tirelessly to improve all important aspects of citizens' rights, such as health, education, taxation, and environmental issues. Being naturally inclined toward foreign affairs, Jimmy brought special envoys and foreign diplomats to Atlanta.

After two years in office, Jimmy decided that it was time that he set his sights on the higher goal of the Presidency. Jimmy's political advisors chalked out various strategies that would help him gain wider recognition in the eyes of the nation. He actively campaigned for Democratic candidates throughout the country, which took him from state to state and gave him the opportunity to interact with more people. Though his family knew of his intention by the end of 1972, Jimmy made public announcements of it only in 1974. The entire Carter family pitched in toward this huge step. All the Carters, including Jimmy's mother, wife, grown-up sons, their wives, his aunts, uncles, and cousins, worked hard toward introducing this not-so-well-known personage to the world at large.

As a team, they focused on keeping it simple and introducing Jimmy as the Governor of Georgia, a farmer, and an ex-naval man who, being a Washington outsider, wanted to bring greater standards to the government. Jimmy's honesty was what they focused on. In times such as those, when the country was still reeling from scandals and scams such as Watergate, Jimmy's fresh and clean image worked in his favor. While introducing himself as the official Democratic candidate, Jimmy's opening line was a testament to his humble origins, "My name is Jimmy Carter and I'm running for president."

20: The Peanut Brigade, a Few Gaffes, and Victory

The election campaign was in full swing, and the Carters had seven campaigns going on in different parts of the country. They convened briefly to exchange news and then again went back to their respective places to meet more people. Along with them, many citizens started traveling at their own expense to meet others and explain to them why Jimmy deserved a chance to be the president. They became known as the "Peanut Brigade."

One of the questions Jimmy was most often asked was about his view on the racial relations between Whites and Blacks and whether he would ensure Blacks were well-represented in his government. Generally, his responses were met with positivity. Only once did Jimmy slip up. When asked about housing facilities for people of different ethnic origins, he said that he thought it was alright for people of a community to stick together. Though the intentions behind his words weren't malicious, they were blown out of proportion so that it made him seem like a pro-segregationist. However, many people like Daddy King, Andy Young, and Benjamin Mays supported him and the controversy died a natural death.

Jimmy's interview with *Playboy*, in which he had intended to say that he wasn't a paragon of virtue himself and that he wouldn't judge others, was similarly another opportunity that the press and his opponents used against him. What was sensationalized was not his message, but his choice of words in saying that he had looked at women lustfully. The interview nearly cost him the election, and suddenly, his family life was dissected, with Rosalynn being bombarded with questions as to whether she trusted her husband with other women.

Thankfully, though, Jimmy's otherwise squeaky-clean image and transparency were able to win the day for him. He won the presidency in 1976, defeating Gerald Ford, Richard Nixon's vice president, who had been sworn into office after his resignation.

21: President Jimmy

The day when Jimmy was sworn into office as the 39th U.S. president was one of the best days of his life. On a cool morning in January 1977, Jimmy and Rosalynn woke up, hardly able to believe that they had made it to Blair House, the presidential guest house until they moved into the White House.

At the Capitol Building, Jimmy was welcomed by a marine band playing the Navy Hymn in honor of his service to the Navy. Jimmy swore his oath on the Bible presented to him by his mother, Lillian. In his hardly-eight-minute speech, he emphasized his dedication to human rights and the eradication of nuclear weaponization.

But what made the crowd gasp in surprise was the Carters' choice of walking down Pennsylvania Avenue to the White House, instead of using the chauffeured limousine waiting to carry them. This was not exactly an impromptu gesture. It was suggested to Jimmy by Senator Proxmire and he agreed that this was a good way of reducing the imperial status associated with a president and a way of demonstrating his faith in the people as far as his security was concerned. Though the people were amazed at his humility, for Jimmy it was the most natural thing on Earth to do.

At the White House, Jimmy was naturally curious to look at his new office, though he did not exactly know where it was in the huge building. Finally, when he saw the Oval Office, he was filled with a sense of disbelief. Overwhelmed by the historical significance of the place, Jimmy wondered at the beds and desks that had once been used by Lincoln, Truman, Roosevelt, and Kennedy.

His words from his diary give us a glimpse into what he was feeling on that first day (Carter, 2010):

I have a feeling of almost unreality about my being president, but also a feeling of both adequacy and determination that I might live up to the historical precedents established by my predecessors. (p. 10)

Now he had become President Jimmy Carter!

Chapter 4:

Leading With Compassion

When Jimmy Carter assumed the role of the president, the faith of the public in American politics had waned considerably owing to the Watergate scandal. It was also a time of economic crunch, high inflation, rising oil prices, changing gender roles fueling more divorces, the continuing Cold War, and post-Vietnam War pessimism. It was no easy feat for anybody to make changes and get work done at such a time, and also have to restore the faith of the people in the government.

Slowly, Congress started working away at issues and goals that were closest to his heart. Not everything was perfect, but he was driven by his faith and optimism, two things that the citizens seemed to lack the most in that era.

22: Amnesty to Draft Evaders

One of the first things that Carter did was to grant pardon to the men who had not taken part in the Vietnam War. When the draft orders came, several of the eligible men had hidden or fled in order not to participate in the war, owing to their ethical and moral concerns against the war. Carter wanted to grant these men a presidential amnesty. When he met war veteran Max Cleland, the latter warned him that this move would not find Carter in favor with the senate members. Carter replied to him with his characteristic cheeriness that even if nobody agreed with him, he was convinced that it was the right thing to do, and the first step toward healing the nation divided over the war.

Initially, as predicted, Carter's action was met with a huge public outroar. People were disappointed that these men who had evaded their public duty were being pardoned. Eventually, however, it was seen more as a strength of his character. It was proof of his convictions in the right causes.

23: A Man of the Masses

Carter wanted to be seen as one among his citizens. Thus, he distanced himself from the frills and trimmings associated with his position. For instance, he would always carry his own suitcase on trips. He did away with the playing of "Hail to the Chief" when he made his appearance. Carter was also clear that he would prefer to continue with his nickname "Jimmy" rather than his more formal baptismal name "James," even for official purposes. He requested the sale of the presidential yacht and for the money to be reimbursed to the government. It was also his wish that his daughter, Amy, attend a public school in Washington D.C., rather than a fancier, and more expensive private one.

Every day, Carter woke up at 6:30 a.m. and spent some time in his office reading the news, going over memos, and attending to them right away. It was observed that he would often spend 12 hours or more daily in the Oval Office. His views and political opinions were probably not laced with diplomacy because of his faith in always endeavoring to do the right thing. Even people who disagreed with his political choices always agreed that he was one of the most hardworking and decent men the president's office had seen.

Carter was also determined to open up the government to media and public scrutiny. He believed that this was the straightforward thing to do. In the first two years of his presidency, he held 41 press conferences and frequent luncheon discussions at the White House for news editors, publishers, and owners and directors of TV and radio stations.

24: Women's and Racial Empowerment

Demographic diversity was one of Carter's priorities. Keeping to his word, Carter appointed more women and colored people to governmental positions. Three women served on his cabinet, and a record of 41 women were appointed as federal judges. He also chose 16 women ambassadors. Similarly, the total number of appointments of Blacks and Hispanics increased many times. Overall, 57 people of color were given jobs. It was during his tenure that the first female Black circuit court judge, the first Hispanic circuit court judge, and the first female Hispanic district court judge were appointed.

Historically, it was a significant achievement because the Carter government inducted more women and people of color into governmental positions than all the previous governments had appointed together.

25: Deregulation of Airline and Home-Brewing Industries

Carter passed the Airline Deregulation Act in 1978. This allowed the airline industry more freedom to set their fares, taking cost and distance into consideration. It also reduced governmental interference in ticket pricing and the entry of new companies into the market. The powers of the government-run Civil Aeronautics Board were to be slowly phased out in the coming years. Demand and supply would now also decide aviation routes throughout the country. In effect, this would mean that the common man was able to fly at cheaper rates and would have more airline companies to choose from. However, governmental control was still exercised over passenger safety.

The beer industry was also likewise deregulated, a first since the 1920 Prohibition Act, which banned its production, selling, distribution, and transportation by home brewers. After the implementation of this deregulation act, home breweries could now buy malt, hops, and yeast for the first time. Over the years, this led to a microbrewery culture that has flourished into the present times.

26: The Energy Crisis

One of the biggest challenges and roadblocks that Carter faced was the energy crisis that hit the nation in the 1970s. His immediate response to this was to reduce the power consumption of the White House. He would personally turn down the thermostat in the rooms and wear sweaters within its walls. He was also instrumental in having solar water heating panels installed, which would reduce the dependence on electricity.

In August 1977, the Department of Energy was formed to address the problems related to the increasing expenditure incurred on gasoline and other forms of energy. This new department was also to study alternative forms of energy that could be put to use so that the US dependence on foreign oil could be reduced.

However, his greatest promise to the American people about forming a comprehensive energy policy would take a lot longer than he intended. Even when it was passed by Congress in late 1978, it was heavily amended. However, it did make progress in reducing the differences between the pricing of gasoline within and outside each state. It also provided tax credits and benefits to those who opted to use non-fossil fuels and encouraged the reduced use of energy. He was one of the first presidents to caution about the climatic implications of the overuse of fossil fuels and to encourage people and companies to conserve energy.

27: Education and Health

Carter felt that education in the country was too important a matter to be scattered across states and their boards. He envisioned a national framework for education. Thus was born the United States Department of Education, which began operating in 1980.

During his tenure, the budget for education was doubled. He also actively promoted President Lyndon B. Johnson's Head Start program, which provided aid to thousands of children from poor-income families to not just continue their studies but also for the education boards and schools to track the nutrition, health, and parental involvement in children's education.

Though not privately supportive of abortion rights for women, owing to his strong religious faith, Carter had to comply with the Roe vs. Wade Case of 1973, in which the Constitution upheld the right to abortion. However, President Carter was equally determined to promote sex education for teenagers, provide adoption facilities, and give women and children medical and financial aid via the Women and Infant Children (WIC) program, which he felt would reduce the reliance on abortion except as a last resort.

The other program that Carter wanted enacted was universal national health insurance. Though his proposal was passed by the Senate, it was defeated in the House. Many were concerned about the cost that such a program would entail as well as the bureaucratic efforts it would involve. Finally, Carter would have to concede his defeat in trying to establish a comprehensive American healthcare system.

The most spectacular of President Carter's achievements revolved around foreign policy—a field he was especially interested in, and which deserves a lengthier elaboration.

Chapter 5:

Carter the Peacemaker

If President Carter is remembered today for something other than his long list of humanitarian efforts post his presidency, it is for the Camp David Accords. The year was 1977 and tensions were mounting in areas surrounding Israel. After the Six-Day War in 1967, Israel had just annexed large portions of land from surrounding regions such as Egypt. More strife between the Jewish state of Israel and the surrounding Arab countries was imminent, and several presidents had tried their hand at bringing peace between the two warring factions, but to no avail. The situation was volatile and failure to negotiate a peace treaty could result in the overthrow of moderate Arab rulers, the rise of Soviet influence in the region, and the spawning of anti-Western terrorist groups. If there was somebody who could bring a change, it was only President Carter.

In November 1977, the president of Egypt, Anwar al-Sadat, finally broke the ice by visiting the Israeli prime minister, Menachem Begin. Jimmy Carter, who was closely following these developments, thought that the time was ripe to put an end to the years of violence both countries had witnessed.

28: Camp David—The Ideal Place to Forge Peace

After he was sworn in, Carter found the tranquility and greenery of Camp David, a forest resort in Maryland, about 70 miles away from Washington D.C., one of the best perquisites of the president's office. For years, the cool green forest, its woody paths, and cozy cabins were used for rest, recreation, diplomatic negotiations, and to plan political strategies.

In fact, Camp David was one of the few privileges that Carter wanted to maintain. He mentions early on in his *White House Diary* how he asked his Budget Manager not to reveal to him the annual cost of maintaining Camp David, as well as not to undertake any more construction on the site so as to retain its pristine charm. The Carters had often used the place to spend a quiet Sunday afternoon with family members to rest away from the media glare. It was an ideal spot also because Carter could get back to Washington, D.C., if any urgent situation arose that required his presence.

One day, as he walked with Rosalynn through the luxuriant paths of Camp David, he hit upon the idea that would change the Middle Eastern situation forever. He suddenly knew that if the Israel–Egypt peace negotiations were to succeed anywhere, then the two leaders ought to bring their discussion to Camp David. President Carter lost no time in inviting Sadat and Begin to Camp David.

29: The Three Men—Diverse yet United in Purpose

On September 5th, 1978, Carter met Sadat first, who seemed like he was in a hurry to reach a settlement with the Israelis. He warned Carter that Begin would not agree so quickly and that the latter would delay the talks as much as possible. Carter's initial impression was that Sadat seemed to want US endorsement and that he approached Begin with suspicion and impatience. It seemed like he was eager and ambitious to acquire a US partnership against Begin. Carter told him that he would have to try to see the issues from the perspective of Begin. Sadat requested a night for rest and he was amenable to Carter meeting Begin on his own on the first day.

When Carter met Begin, he knew instantly that this was a man of a different mettle. Begin was interested in the procedures that they would follow at Camp David—at what times the meetings would be held, the venues of these meetings, the aides who would join them, and so forth. He reminded Carter that it was unprecedented for an Israeli leader to establish an agreement with Egyptians and that it had not happened over the last two thousand years. He wanted to jump right in and begin discussions on Lebanon that very night. But when informed of Sadat's request, he acquiesced.

Carter would find during the course of the discussions that Sadat was easily angered, and at a moment's notice, he would threaten to withdraw from the peace talks. Several times during the next grueling 13 days, the talks broke down, only to be picked up again. Begin, on the other hand, was calm and yet inflexible about the Israeli position. He talked like countless hard-line Israeli leaders before him and picked on every single line of the agreement document. From the outset, it was clear that Begin would be a tough customer to please.

Carter was also privately amused at the difference in attitude of the two men. While Sadat laid down terms that everyone, including himself, knew the Israelis wouldn't accept, he also made it clear that he was open to negotiations and modifications on many aspects. On the other hand, Begin's stand was the same in public or private and he found it hard to comprehend why an honorable man would publicly say something and then privately another.

The stress on Carter was unimaginable as he tried to bring peace, justice, and fairness into the equation while maintaining the US stance of noninterference.

30: The Talks

Carter had supposed that the Camp David talks would last for a maximum of five days, and yet it stretched on because both sides could not come to an agreement on many points, including the governance of disputed lands and the question of Jerusalem. There were several times when Sadat nearly walked out and Carter had to restrain him and appeal to his better judgment. Heated discussions were followed by stilted conversations that did little by way of making any progress.

On day six, which was a Sunday, Carter suggested that the entire team visit the historic Gettysburg Plains, where Lincoln had famously delivered his address. His only stipulation was that no political discussions would be made that day and that it was only to be a day of respite. During the drive, Carter deliberately sat between the two men, trying to drive a peaceful conversation. Most of the officials were excited about this trip and were animatedly chattering away, but Begin was quiet. However, when they reached the site, Begin was mumbling something and the whole group went silent when they realized that he was quoting Lincoln's entire speech verbatim.

There was a lingering sense of hope, as Sadat, referencing how the North and South of America had healed to form the USA, said how he envisaged the same for Israel–Egypt relations.

31: The Accords—Peace at Last

The Camp David peace treaty draft, which was titled *A Framework for Peace in the Middle East*, was revised several times over the course of discussions and even then, it did not address many issues on which both of the leaders would not budge. For instance, there was still no clarity over the question of who would control Jerusalem, which was holy to Christians, Muslims, and Jews. However, Egypt recognized the legitimacy of the Israeli government and Israel returned the lands it had seized from Egypt and other Arab nations.

On day 11 of the talks, Carter had to personally intervene and talk with Sadat about why he would endanger his relationship both with Israel and with the US if he chose to abandon the negotiations at this stage. He saw how Sadat froze at the seriousness of his tone and voice. Carter also renewed his promises to the Egyptians and promised them wheat and corn, because food was in short supply in Egypt. After having settled matters, the two men watched a heavyweight fight between Muhammed Ali and Spinks.

On day 13, Carter made it clear to both leaders that whether they reached an agreement or not, the talks would have to be concluded as he needed to get back to his duties as the president of America.

An interesting episode led to the final signing of the treaty. Carter and Begin were exchanging signed photographs for their families. Carter had instructed his staff to have each of the photos handed over to Begin personalized with the names of his grandchildren. When Begin saw how the photos had the names of all his grandchildren, he went over them carefully, one at a time. His eyes went misty. Both the men got emotional as they shared stories about families during the war.

Initially, though Begin said that he wouldn't relent on his stand, peace was eventually achieved. One of the final points for clinching the treaty was Israel's decision to withdraw its troops from Sinai, rehabilitate existing civilian citizens, and prohibit new settlements from arising there, with the intention of handing back the lands to Egypt.

Finally, the treaty was passed and 30 years of war and travel restrictions between Egypt and Israel ended. The agreement between the leaders was signed at the White House on the same day. It was a historic win for the world and specifically for Carter.

32: The Aftermath—Not all Rosy

Though it was one of the largest feathers in Carter's cap, not everyone viewed the Camp David Accords in the same way. The UN, for instance, was not happy about being excluded from the entire process. After some deliberation, it was announced that the peace treaty would be considered null and void by the UN General Assembly because it did not mention the Palestinian right of return and sovereignty. In 1979, the UN further condemned the continued occupation of Palestine by Israel. However, as far as Middle-Eastern politics and peace is concerned every negotiation harks back to the Camp David Accords as a starting point even today.

Though Sadat and Begin were jointly awarded the Nobel Peace Prize in 1978, both were criticized in their own countries for being part of this international treaty. Begin was censured by his own party for endangering Israel's security, while Sadat had literally turned all the Arab nations against himself and Egypt. Egypt was suspended from the Arab League from 1979–'89. Sadat was eventually assassinated three years later by a fundamentalist group within his own country.

By the time Sadat was killed, Carter was no longer the president. Ronald Reagan, the new president, never attended the funeral owing to security concerns. However, his three immediate predecessors—Nixon, Ford, and Carter paid homage to Sadat. During the interview that he gave with the press, Carter admitted that not including the Saudis and Jordanians in Camp David was perhaps a mistake in hindsight. He also felt that Sadat's courage had made him a pariah among the other Arab countries (*Carter and Ford*, 1981).

Though his involvement in the Camp David Accords threw Carter more than ever into the limelight, this wasn't his only diplomatic victory. There have been several others that definitely contributed to making the world a more harmonious place to live in.

Chapter 6:

Other Diplomatic Successes

Even as a boy, Jimmy loved to hear anecdotes about other lands and how people lived there. When his uncle Tom used to send him postcards from ports across the globe, young Jimmy swore that he, too, would travel the world one day as a naval officer. As the President, Carter did not travel for leisure exactly, but as the harbinger of peace. Here, we look at Carter's legacy in certain peace negotiations and treaties in which he played a huge role.

33: The Panama Canal Treaties

The Panama Canal was strategically very important to the US because it allowed for easy crossing between the Atlantic and Pacific Oceans, especially for trade and war. The canal itself was built by America in 1914 and was controlled by the US. However, Panamanians had come to dislike and resent the US presence in what they believed was rightfully their territory.

Earlier Presidents, including Nixon, had sought to end the problem by negotiating a deal that was favorable to both the US and Panama. By the time Carter assumed the post, things had come to such a head that a rebellion was imminent. Carter had to act and he had to act fast. He met several times with the Panamanian President Omar Torrijos.

Two treaties were signed as a result of these interactions. The first one allowed for the gradual release of the canal's control to Panama by the end of 1999. The second treaty, which was valid forever, was to ensure the neutrality of the canal during both peace and war times.

Even though the two treaties were signed, Carter still had hard work ahead of him in getting Congress to pass it. Conservative Republicans and many other Americans saw the canal as a part of America's glorious past. They were reluctant to let go of the control of the tiny strip of land. They felt that the President had acted against the interest of the country.

However, this was where Carter's diplomatic brilliance and oratorical abilities came into play. Finally, after much debate, he got the necessary ratification and the treaties were brought into effect in 1978.

34: SALT

The Strategic Arms Limitation Talks I (SALT) were already set in motion by the previous President, Gerald Ford, with the Soviet President Leonid Brezhnev. This was a diplomatic attempt to reduce the nuclear arms race on both sides and, thus, to prevent the world from another attack such as Hiroshima and Nagasaki during WWII. Per the terms of SALT I signed in 1972, neither the US nor the Soviet Union were supposed to build any new weapons for a period of five years.

Carter came into office when SALT I had just about expired. He wanted to attempt to further reduce the danger of nuclear weapons by signing SALT II with the Soviets. He worked closely with his political advisors on the best terms for such an agreement so that both parties would decrease the number and complexity of nuclear weapons, and so that they would freeze or slow down the development of such weapons.

If Carter feared that the Soviets would dissent and oppose SALT II, the main protest for it came from Congress, which largely felt that SALT II would weaken the American defense system.

Carter met with Brezhnev. Being a plainspoken man, Carter minced no words in telling the Soviets that they were much too harsh on the dissidents within their nation and that human rights violation in the

Soviet Union was something that the US could not close its eyes to. Brezhnev and the other Russian diplomats were displeased with what they saw as US interference in their internal affairs. However, SALT II was finally signed by the two sides in June 1979. The euphoria over this achievement was short-lived.

A combination of many events would eventually lead to SALT II not being implemented. For one thing, it wasn't ratified by the Senate. Secondly, in December 1979, the Soviets invaded Afghanistan, where the earlier pro-Soviet government was overturned by Muslim rebels. Carter condemned the Soviet invasion of Afghanistan and relations between the two world powers broke down once more. Carter has often maintained that his failure to get the Senate to pass SALT II and its subsequent withdrawal was one of the bitterest disappointments he faced as a president and as a peace lover.

35: The Olympic Boycott and Embargoes on the Soviet Union

Though 1978 and '79 had witnessed the Carter government trying to improve its bonds with the Soviet Union, by December, the latter's invasion of Afghanistan ended these attempts. Carter was vociferous about his government's distaste for human rights violations. He reciprocated with strong and swift action, such as postponing the inauguration of a new Soviet embassy in New York. He suspended the export of wheat and other grains to the USSR, which partially backfired as losses for American farmers. Arts exchanges between the two countries were suspended.

The boldest and most definitive move, however, was Carter's decision to boycott the Moscow Olympics of 1980. Other countries like China and Japan followed suit and refrained from sending their players. It was not just athletes, but also US technology and other goods necessary for conducting the Olympics that were barred entry into the Soviet Union. He also convinced NBC not to pay the outstanding $20 million to the Soviets to broadcast the Olympics.

At home, 73% of Americans approved of Carter's decision with regard to the embargo.

36: China

During Carter's reign, he strengthened relations with Communist China. In fact, the Chinese government was diplomatically recognized in 1979, at the cost of severing ties with noncommunist Taiwan, which had always been politically at loggerheads with the mainland. Granting recognition to China eased the tension in East Asia and mutually beneficial US–China trade relations could be established. The US exported lumber and food and imported a variety of consumer goods from China.

Just as with his other policies, Congress opposed the recognition granted to a communist country and was skeptical that US trading ties with Taiwan would cease, causing economic problems for the country. However, their fears remained unfounded because the US–Taiwan association was maintained via external organizations and channels. The US continued supplying arms to Taiwan to defend itself against China as before.

The Carters invited the Chinese Vice Premier Deng Xiaoping and his wife to the US, during which time the latter stayed in the White House for three days. The president would go on to establish a personal relationship with Xiaoping in the coming years.

37: Africa

In contrast to the policies of earlier presidents, Carter was much more attuned to the problems in Africa. He was one of the first sitting Presidents to visit sub-Saharan Africa. One of the primary reasons for this policy shift was also because of Andrew Young, the first Black American ambassador to the UN.

The Carter regime was heavily critical of African countries that had predominantly White governments, such as Rhodesia and South Africa. Carter lobbied for fair elections in these countries and for more Black representation in their administrations. He also condemned the continued racial segregation in South Africa via apartheid and the country's illegal occupation of Namibia. Carter enforced an arms embargo against South Africa.

In Rhodesia, the US played a crucial role in the transition from the White government to the Black people's government and the subsequent formation of Zimbabwe.

38: South Korea

Historically speaking, South Korea had always been a US ally. However, Carter was so incensed at the human rights violations against protestors within the country that he threatened to withdraw American troops stationed there to protect the country against North Korea. But he never got the support of the other congressional members for it. Japan was also against this move. Carter could only withdraw a token number of the American troops in South Korea.

Eventually, the South Korean president was assassinated and General Chun Doo-hwan overtook the governance of the country. Carter eventually had to provide support to the newly established regime in control. A complete removal of troops from South Korea never took place, though America's continued presence in South Korea helped it to resist an invasion by the Soviet-backed North Korea.

39: Carter Doctrine

This was Carter's answer to the Soviet crisis in Afghanistan. He said that the presence of Soviets in Afghanistan, a mere 300 miles from the Indian Ocean and close to the straits of Hormuz, from where the world's oil flowed, posed a grave threat to the free movement of oil from the Middle East. He further said that any threat to the oil from the Persian Gulf region was a direct threat against the US and the world, which would be remedied by military force if needed.

In implementation, this was the beginning of the Rapid Deployment Force, which later became the US Central Command (CENTCOM) deployed in the Middle East, and Central and South Asia. Selective Service registration for civilian conscription was restarted, as well as an increase in defense expenditure. The US Naval presence in the Gulf region was increased, too.

Ronald Reagan extended the Carter Doctrine in 1981 into what was often termed "Reagan's Corollary to the Carter Doctrine," though, in principle, it was very much similar in theme. This paved the way for Operation Desert Storm during the Gulf War of 1991.

40: Nicaragua

Carter went against tradition at times in keeping with his values. He ended years of US diplomatic ties with one of the most brutal rulers of Latin America, President Somoza of Nicaragua, who was once famous for having said, "I don't want an educated population; I want oxen" (gordonskene, 2019). This government was as corrupt as it was cruel to its subjects. There is evidence to suggest that the president himself was involved in the export of imported blood plasma for earthquake victims in the country. Somoza's close aides were involved in the embezzlement of humanitarian funds that flowed into the country as well. The Catholic church also opposed Somoza's inhuman rule. Human rights groups had started rallying against the government.

Eventually, Somoza's government fell to a rebel group within the country. He fled with most of the Nicaraguan national treasure. The next rulers found little more than $2 million in the treasury, while the country had accrued a whopping $1.6 billion in foreign debts. President Carter refused to give Somoza asylum in the US. The latter had to turn to Paraguay for help, where he was killed by his political enemies a year later.

Though Carter had the zeal of a missionary and the vision of an idealist, he often could not do everything he wanted to, because his hands were tied by Congress and dissenting Senate members who, though from his own party, were at times more conservative in their ideology. His tenure was marked by this rift with Congress from beginning to end. Since we have looked at his political and foreign policy successes, we shall also look at some of the biggest internal and external challenges Carter faced, and, more importantly, how he dealt with them and how they shaped him.

Chapter 7:

Surmounting Challenges

Carter's initial popularity waned as time went on. This was not necessarily because he did not meet expectations as a president, but because the times were hard and people always sought a scapegoat to blame their troubles on. Not everyone understood Carter's idealistic honesty or his spiritual faith and optimism. He had dissidents both within the party and outside who were quick to label his warm and open nature as a publicity stunt.

Apart from a growing unease with the economic situation of the country, Carter had to face tricky foreign relations problems as well.

41: Uganda and Idi Amin

Carter had, as usual, condemned the cruel dictator of Uganda, Idi Amin, for reports of government brutality. Idi Amin responded by calling all Americans in Uganda for a meeting with him in Entebbe. He then proceeded to single out a hundred White missionaries and told them that he would execute them one by one unless Carter apologized to him within a specified period of time.

President Carter, who was at the time enjoying quiet family time in Camp David, immediately called the Saudi Arabian King, who was an ally and who might help in communicating matters to a fellow Muslim ruler like Amin. Though the Saudi King helped, Carter still had to apologize for his words, even though he knew that he hadn't been wrong in criticizing the many human rights violations in Uganda. Idi Amin, thankfully, relented and then told the American missionaries that they were free to leave Uganda if they chose to.

To Carter's pride, most of the missionaries bravely chose to stay back and continue God's work.

42: Deployment of the Neutron Bomb

Carter agreed to technological advancement in defense on the whole. However, when he was told about the neutron bomb that would significantly decrease the loss of property but would be lethal to people owing to its deadly radiation, he wasn't convinced if it was something that either America or NATO should deploy. It had already been tested in 1963 and the military was aiming for production when Carter decided to advise for its ban. Many European leaders agreed with Carter. But the German Chancellor Schmidt was angry at what he saw as a refusal to avail of a good weapon. He publicly criticized Carter, who replied that he would reconsider his decision if the Chancellor agreed to deploy the neutron bomb in Germany. As Carter had assumed rightly, Schmidt was unwilling to partake of this responsibility and its deployment was stalled. President Reagan sanctioned the use of this weapon, and though it was used for a while in the U.S. defense, the last one was dismantled during the presidency of George W. Bush.

43: The Chrysler Question

Chrysler Corporation, one of the biggest defense contractors for the federal government, was running into big losses and faced the possibility of insolvency. Lee Iacocca, the new CEO, approached the Carter government for help. Carter proposed a huge bailout program for the company, which employed 1,650 Americans. The other issue was that if the government refused aid, Chrysler faced the prospect of being taken over by willing and aggressive Japanese automobile companies. To prevent all of these from happening, Carter sanctioned a $1.5 billion guaranteed loan, which had to be repaid by the company once it got back on its feet. Carter ensured that Chrysler adhered to conditions for strict operations practices and labor union concessions, which were overseen by the treasury secretary. The company was also held to full repayment of the loan at the then-interest rate. When it recovered, the government benefited greatly from this intervention.

44: The Royal Crown of Hungary

This was a decision that seemed natural and fair to Carter and yet was surprisingly met with overwhelming criticism. The Royal Crown of Hungary had been with the US for several years. This crown was a part of Hungarian heritage. It was handed down to the first Hungarian king by the Catholic Pope in the year 1000. It was called the Crown of Saint Stephen. During WWII, when Hungary was invaded by the soviet troops, faithful Hungarians, responsible for the protection of the crown, handed it over to the U.S. troops for safekeeping. It had since then been kept at Fort Knox along with the American national gold.

Carter felt that it was only right for the Hungarians to have their crown back. However, Hungary was, at the time, still under Soviet rule. People assumed that Carter was "weak" in handing over this treasure to the communists. Hungarian-Americans were also angry that Carter should "disrespect" the wishes of their parent country. Carter returned it in 1978, on the grounds that the crown and insignia must be controlled and protected by Hungarians and be allowed to be displayed as early as it was practically possible.

A duplicate of the crown was handed back to Carter for his gesture in 1998. This twin of the crown is on display today at the Presidential Museum.

In 1996, when the Carters went to Hungary as part of their humanitarian efforts, they visited the Hungarian National Museum, where they saw the crown again. Carter was told that three million people annually visit it, some of them even offering their prayers to it. The crown was eventually moved to the Hungarian Parliament Building, where it resides to this day.

45: Alaska

Alaska, though inducted as the 49th state in 1959, still faced the question of how its lands would be divided between Native Americans and Eskimos. The two options were to either deed the lands to the state government of Alaska or to retain them as national forests, parks, and reserves. A further complication was the discovery of oil there and the boom in commercial fisheries. Alaska was now a wealthy state and nobody wanted to make a final decision on the matter.

The rich oil lobby did not want the lands to be marked as national reserves because that would cut into their profits. Environmentalists and natives were supportive of Carter's plan to convert Alaskan lands to protected sites. After studying the matter thoroughly, Carter's secretary of interior came up with a plan. They decided to invoke the Antiquities Act of 1906, by which a president could call for the demarcation and setting aside of land that contained ancient burial grounds, Indian artifacts, or other monuments of historical significance. Using this, Carter got large portions of land declared as "national monuments" worthy of preservation and protection. Almost 56 million acres of land were declared to be protected land.

Of course, within Alaska, Carter was hated by hunters, loggers, fishers, and industrialists. Whenever he visited the state, he had to have added security. At the state fair of Alaska, a game of target shooting allowed visitors to throw baseballs at two targets, which would dunk a clown in water. One of the targets had Carter's face, while the other had that of the Iranian president, Ayatollah Khomeini. Carter remembers that few people threw at Khomeini.

46: Native American Settlements in Maine

An interesting legal problem faced Carter in the form of claims from Native Americans who felt they owned about 12.5 million acres, which was then under the control of about 350,000 Whites. The Maine

Congressional delegation was in support of paying off the claimants with a fixed land value as in 1976, without any interest added, while the Interior Department sympathized with the indigenous people.

Carter asked for the help and intervention of the retired chief justice of the Georgia Supreme Court, William Gunter. The final decision was made based on his recommendation. As it was an important subject for Maine, many politicians and intellectuals got involved in the debate. The final papers toward the settlement were signed by the president in 1980. Eighty-one and a half million dollars was used to purchase the title to 305,000 acres of woodland and to provide close to $27 million in a trust fund for the Native American tribes. As a result, each member of the tribe got $25,000 and 275 acres of land.

47: The Commemoration of Dylan Thomas

When Carter went to England for a summit with six other global leaders, he wanted to visit Laugharne, the Welsh home of Dylan Thomas, his favorite poet. But other responsibilities got in the way and Carter could not go. When at Westminster Abbey, Carter visited the poet's corner and asked the archbishop for the place where Dylan Thomas was honored. The archbishop said that Thomas was too disreputable to be included in the Poet's Corner.

Carter went on to argue about the characters of other poets who were also deemed to be social misfits during their times, such as Byron and Poe. This was reported widely by the press and Thomas' widow wrote to Carter thanking him for his support for her late husband.

Carter's advisors warned him that the subject would bring no results and that he was wasting his time and probably angering authorities by questioning their decision not to honor Dylan Thomas. But Carter remained firm, and when he returned to Washington, D.C., he wrote a letter to the archbishop and his committee praising the poet's extraordinary talent. Wonderful as it may seem, during Carter's last week in office, it was decided that Dylan Thomas would be commemorated in the Poet's Corner. Carter recorded a message that was played at the ceremony by the BBC. Happy citizens of Laugharne later sent him a miniature of the stone marker in honor of the poet in Westminster, which he could display in the presidential library.

48: B-1 Bombers

As early as when the election campaign was happening, Carter knew that he would have to take a final call on the building of the B-1 bomber aircraft. Once he was elected, Carter set a deadline for June 1977 and took the opinion of advisors and defense personnel on whether these new planes needed to be deployed at all. Finally, Carter decided that there was no real need to undertake the production of this extremely expensive aircraft and that they could manage for the present with B-52s and smaller airplanes, with the addition of high-precision cruise missiles that could be fired from land, submarines, and other vessels. The development of stealth technology was also making it possible for B-2 bombers and other aircraft to be invisible on enemy radars—a feature that was soon to be implemented.

The move not to build B-1 bombers was passed by the Senate and Congress with little disagreement. However, defense contractors were sorely disappointed by the move. When Reagan became the president, he sanctioned the production of a hundred B-1s at a cost of $200 million each. Time would prove this an unnecessary cost as upgraded B-52s still continue in service and are expected to do so until 2040 and the B-2 until 2058.

49: Cabinet Reorganization

One of the first things that Carter did when he became the president was also one of his decisions that drew a lot of censure. He wanted to "simplify" and "streamline" the government. But no Democrat wanted to introduce the bill, because the chairman of the Government

Operations Committee, who was influential, deemed the move "unconstitutional."

Carter took his ideas to the Republicans, who were more favorably disposed to them. The bill was passed in early 1977. During his presidency, Carter proposed 11 recommendations and 10 of them were accepted and passed. He was also instrumental in the creation of two new cabinet departments, which incorporated or led to the dismantling of smaller departments from earlier that weren't as effective. The two new ones were the Energy and Education departments. These departments, though threatened to be knocked down by subsequent presidents several times, have survived to today.

Sad as Carter was about the intense opposition to ideas, he thought were straightforward and fairly commonsensical, there were also decisions that were taken in good faith but backfired. In the next chapter, we look at some instances of external and internal affairs that led to Carter's defeat in the 1980 presidential elections.

Chapter 8:

Lessons From Defeat

Perhaps Carter learned more from his defeats than all his victories put together. As a farmer from humble origins, and as a president who wanted to do so much good that it sometimes ached that nobody seemed to be on his page, he has definitely undergone his share of woes. Here, we look at some of the personal and political failures that dogged Carter and what he learned from them.

50: Missed Rhodes Scholarship

When he was fresh out of the Naval Academy, a young Jimmy applied for the prestigious Rhodes Scholarship to study at Oxford. He took a lot of pains over this endeavor and got the requisite endorsement and letters of recommendation from the staff of the Naval Academy and elsewhere. He wrote his essay and submitted it as a citizen of Georgia. He took pains to keep abreast of both historical and current political affairs of significance and read up on everything he believed would be important toward securing the scholarship. He wanted nothing more than to use his experience as a naval officer to study international affairs and then to work for world peace.

Jimmy almost secured it, too. He was invited to Atlanta for an interview with the selection committee. His main contender was a young literature scholar from Alabama whose area of expertise was Elizabethan literature. In fact, this man had said that nothing beyond the period of Queen Elizabeth I, who died in 1603, interested him. Jimmy was asked questions on history, geography, politics, and current affairs, all of which he successfully answered. So thorough was his preparation.

However, when the final result came the scholar from Alabama got the scholarship. This was indeed a crushing blow to Jimmy, who had prepared well and who must have secretly at least thought that his subjects were far more useful to the world than the scholar's interest in the Elizabethan period.

He kept up a correspondence with the young man via letters for a while. Later, he learned that the young man had died while still a student in England. Though he had not known him well, he was grieved at the loss of the man's parents and that a life had been cut short in the bloom of youth.

51: Giving Up the Naval Career

Though we gave a brief description of Jimmy's exit from the Navy earlier, we did not go into the matter and the months of moral and ethical conundrum it put Jimmy in. On the one hand, he was drawn to his family business and a dying father's work. On the other hand, Jimmy was establishing a budding career in the Navy and he was mounting the ladder of success one step at a time. Induction into Rickover's project was one of the finest moments of Jimmy's life. Add to that the fact that his family was just finding its feet after years of scraping together a living. Finally, they had the money and the respect that they had worked so hard toward. Rosalynn was enjoying her freedom as the wife of a naval officer and she had her own way of running her household, which now included their three boys.

Thus, when Jimmy decided after his father's funeral that he would take over the business, one from which he had been away for 12 years, it was with trepidation and anxiety that he viewed it. And yet, as a good son and family man, Jimmy was also convinced that it was his responsibility. Rosalynn did not favor the decision. In fact, she was furious with Jimmy, who seemed to be throwing away a good life and career on the gamble that the farmlands would do well and give them enough to sustain their growing family. Even on their journey back home, Rosalynn refused to talk to Jimmy, using their eldest son as an intermediary to convey her needs to her husband. Of course, eventually, she would understand his decision and support him, but that came later.

When Jimmy put in his resignation, he was just as glad as he was guilty. And though Rickover never brought it up, his disdain for Jimmy's decision was evident.

52: Running for Governorship

The first time Jimmy ran for the governor's office in 1966, he had assumed that his good nature and intentions would win him the office. It was not that Jimmy was naive, but he was sure that a man such as Lester Maddox, who was a known segregationist and one who had actually banned Black people from entering his restaurant by arming himself and blocking the door, ought not to become governor.

It wasn't just the loss of governorship, but that he lost to such a man as Maddox that drove Jimmy to desperation. He couldn't understand how the people could vote for such a person. Georgia, after the election, was dubbed "Maddox Country," much to the embarrassment of liberals like Jimmy.

Jimmy was, in fact, so crushed by the defeat that he took his family and drove away into the night without waiting to thank his campaign workers. The action could have been misconstrued as egoistical or ungrateful. However, Hamilton Jordan, who was Jimmy's chief campaign volunteer and worked closely with Jimmy, wondered whether the latter had been crying. But two weeks later, Jimmy called back, apologizing for having left without thanking him, and then broached the more serious subject of whether Jordan would help him again to win the next governor's elections to be held in 1970.

53: Loss of Faith and the Gain of It

After the loss in the election, Jimmy suffered a brief period of disillusionment and possible depression. In his own words, he has said that nothing he did brought any gratification and he felt miserable when he failed at something (Morris, 1996). He had turned back to farming and though there wasn't any financial trouble as such for the Carters, Jimmy felt unfulfilled and lost. He also says of this period how he felt self-loathing and was overcome by his pride.

In the autumn of that year, he took a walk through the woods with his sister Ruth, who had battled her own depression and became a faith healer and evangelical born-again. She talked to Jimmy about how he should surrender himself to the Lord. Somewhere in those woods, Jimmy knew that he should recommit to God, religion, and faith. Though he has always been embarrassed to talk at length about it, Jimmy's experience was transformative. For a while, he set aside political ambitions and focused on his work and "pioneer missions." Jimmy and others like him started their work in Lock Haven, Pennsylvania, where they were to meet families that were recognized to be not very religious, meet them in person, and talk to them about their faith. Jimmy's group was low on funds and they only had access to the telephone, at night and during the weekends.

The aim was not to "convert" these families. Jimmy, who was used to winning and achieving his goals, found it rather strange that they would just do their best and then leave it to the Holy Spirit as to whether these families embraced their message or not.

Jimmy met with people who would not receive them, those who treated the whole thing as a joke, and yet others who seemed to be desperately waiting for the message they were bringing to them. On the whole, the experience gave Jimmy back what he had lost: his faith. Political commentators and people who worked with Jimmy Carter closely always maintained that his political vision and zeal were marked by an underlying spiritual faith.

54: Cuba

One of the political impasses that faced Carter was his relationship with Fidel Castro, the leader of Cuba. America had difficulties with Cuba historically, which was compounded by the country's communist leanings and close ties with the Soviet Union. Diplomatic ties had ceased between the two countries since 1961. Carter wanted to ease the trade embargoes imposed on Cuba, and the travel restrictions so that Americans could travel to Cuba. However, he was also clear that it was time for Cuba to release several Americans who were imprisoned there as "political prisoners."

Initially, Castro was unwilling to agree to any kind of settlement. He, too, wanted trade and travel restrictions lifted, but without any reciprocatory steps from his side. Eventually, American travel to Cuba was enabled and the US–Cuba maritime and fisheries agreement was signed. In 1978, Castro released around 3,600 prisoners, who were screened and about 1,000 of them were accepted back into the US.

However, the ties were again strained by Cuba's continued involvement in the Ethiopian crisis, and their inability to withdraw their troops from Ethiopia owing to their subservience to the Soviets. The situation was worsened by the Mariel Boatlift incident, where Cuba sent boatloads of criminals along with legitimate immigrants to American shores.

Carter, who had always wanted to straighten out ties with Cuba, was unable to make any headway in the matter.

55: Women's Rights

Something that greatly saddened Carter was the opposition that he faced while trying to champion women's rights. From the outset, he had actively sought to increase political positions and other rights for women and minority groups within the country. This is why he had increased the number of women, Blacks, and people of the Latino community appointed to governmental positions. He also pushed for the Equal Rights Amendment (ERA), which would guarantee that "equality of rights under the law shall not be denied or abridged by the United States or by any state on account of sex."

You would think that it would be men who would oppose such an amendment. To Carter's surprise, the biggest backlash came from women led by Phyllis Schlafly, who alleged that equality for women would endanger the laws that protected them. He noted that most of her speeches began with her thanking her husband for giving her permission to talk.

There were also dramatic events, such as a threat from the president of the National Organization of Women to chain herself to the fence around the White House. This was to protest against Carter's personal views against abortion. Interestingly, though he has always been against abortion on moral and religious grounds, as a president, he backed the constitution, which, at the time, upheld abortion rights for women within the first three months of pregnancy. His greatest conflict as a president was his stance on abortion. He tried to resolve this by reducing the number of abortions in the country by educating people and families about the use of contraceptives, family planning, and the economic viability of having a baby. He also tried to make adoptions smoother for the birth and adoptive mothers.

56: Waning Popularity—"Mush From the Wimp"

A rather embarrassing incident happened toward the end of Jimmy Carter's presidency. *The Boston Globe* reported on a speech that Carter delivered in 1980. The article wasn't exactly critical about the president. The gist of the article was Carter's words on economic discipline for the people because of the rising inflation. However, the editorial writer, Kirk Scharfenberg, wasn't very impressed with Carter's "wishy-washy" speech, as he termed it. As an in-house joke, he had titled the article as "More Mush From the Wimp," which was to be removed before the article was published and replaced with the more politically correct "All Must Share the Burden."

Due to an oversight, 161,000 copies of the article were printed and circulated on March 15, 1980, before the mistake was noticed. The newspaper agency issued a public apology to the president and reprinted the correct heading in the subsequent editions.

But the damage had been done. The insulting term was often whipped out against Carter during the election campaign that followed, and alongside his waning popularity, his perception as a "wimp" was sealed in the public consciousness. Ronald Reagan may never have called Carter a wimp to his face, and yet, as he continued to harp on the inefficiency and ineffectiveness of Carter's presidency, the public continued to equate it with the headline.

57: The Killer Bunny Episode

In April 1979, as Jimmy Carter was fishing in a small boat in Plains, a swamp rabbit, which was being chased by hounds and possibly rabid, jumped into the river and swam toward his boat. Carter did not want to harm the creature and yet was sure that if unhindered it would jump into his boat and might bite him. He managed to use his oar to splash water onto the rabbit, which swam away. Later, he happened to mention this story to his staff, including Jody Powell, who was his press secretary, a couple of months later. Everyone treated it as a joke, some even being incredulous that a rabbit should swim.

Powell mentioned this story to one of his journalist friends, not with any malicious intent, but merely for conversation's sake. What followed was relentless humiliation and trolling of the president in columns, cartoons, and articles in the newspapers. For instance, *The Washington Post* carried a first-page article with the title "Bunny Goes Bugs: Rabbit Attacks President." The initial article that was published did not really intend to make fun of the president, but it soon turned into a media circus. People debated if the president's act of splashing water onto the rabbit was a display of his "weakness" and whether it foreshadowed his "timidity" in the wake of the Iran hostage crisis and so on. In his autobiography, Powell expressed his intense regret that he had ever leaked the story to the press, even if it was unwittingly (Powell, 1984).

The incident was all but forgotten when Reagan moved into the White House. His staff found photographs confirming what Carter had said. Pictures of him in a boat and a white rabbit swimming away were indeed found. They released it to the press and the furor over it started all over again.

58: The Iran Hostage Crisis

This was the defining disaster that led to Carter's defeat in the 1980 elections against Reagan. Iran was undergoing political upheaval. The ruling Shah, who was pro-American, cracked down on dissidents and banished them. One among those who were captured and exiled in 1963 was Ayatollah Khomeini, a right-wing religious leader and nationalist. The Shah's Westernizing influence was resented by many in the country. When it was clear that an uprising was imminent, the Shah fled from Iran in 1979. The Ayatollah returned in the political vacuum and stirred up discontent against the Shah and America.

Later, when the Shah approached the US for his cancer treatment, Carter was torn. On the one hand, the Shah had been an ally, and on the other, he knew that it would create further trouble with Iran. However, he finally decided to allow the Shah to be admitted to a facility in the country. The Iranians were so incensed that their enemy was being granted asylum by the US, that they overran and captured the U.S. embassy in Tehran on November 4th, 1979. Around 70 Americans were taken hostage. This situation lasted for 444 days.

Meanwhile, Carter tried his best to talk and sort out the issue diplomatically. He also threatened Iran with embargoes and other actions if the Americans were not returned. Even so, Iran persisted. Carter said clearly that if any of the taken were harmed, military retaliation from the US would be swift. This ensured that Iran took care of the safety of the hostages.

Five months into the hostage crisis, America decided to launch a rescue operation involving planes to overwhelm the rebel group at Tehran. But an untoward accident thwarted the mission, killing eight of the servicemen. Finally, the other planes returned home, aborting the mission. Since Carter was loath to use military force against Iran, the hostage crisis dragged on and his popularity in America waned day by day. Reagan and other political opponents used this episode against Carter to highlight the "weakness" of his leadership. It worked because the public turned toward the more charismatic Reagan.

59: The 1980 Elections

To put matters in perspective, Ronald Reagan was an ex-actor. He knew how to leverage his acting skills to win people over. He was warm, friendly, humorous, and a man of action. He used the lull in popularity that Carter was experiencing to his benefit, losing no opportunity to frame the peace-loving Carter as a dithering leader, incapable of making decisions. Reagan also knew how to read the changing tastes of the public and allied himself with rising conservatives, who were against abortions and homosexuality. To make matters worse was the ongoing Iran hostage crisis which dragged on for more than a year. This was enough for the public. Though Reagan never gave clear answers to many of the burning political problems, the people were dazzled by his smile and charm. Reagan's question to the public was whether they were better off than they were four years ago when Carter had just been sworn in. It was a clever tactic because, using that one question, he managed to question and undermine all the good that Carter had done for the country. It also avoided discussions about how difficult the Carter era had been on the whole in terms of managing national debts, economic depression, and inflation.

The last year before the 1980 elections was really tough on Carter. In fact, he hadn't gone home for Christmas to Plains, a long-standing tradition. He had also taken to sleeping in the Oval Office so that he could be available at a moment's notice in case there was a development in Iran. He did not really campaign at all for the election owing to the same reason.

The final nail in Carter's presidential coffin and possibly the cruelest insult that was dealt to him was the fact that the Iranian hostages were freed by the Ayatollah on the day Reagan became president! Carter never participated in Reagan's swearing-in ceremony. He was on a plane to a military hospital in West Germany where the freed American hostages were being treated.

Chapter 9:

Humanitarian Efforts

Ask any average American and they will probably tell you that Carter is a better person than he was a president. Well, we may not be the best judges of that statement, and yet, we cannot ignore the enormous amount of good that Carter has done for the world through his association with charitable institutions such as the Carter Center and Habitat for Humanity. In this section, we will look at just a few of the milestones that Carter's humanitarian efforts have achieved and why it was only right that he was awarded the Nobel Peace Prize in 2002.

60: The Carter Center

It was on a night after they exited the White House that Rosalynn found Carter sitting up in bed deep in thought. She asked him what was the matter, and he told her that he had hit upon the right plan to continue his work after the presidency. He told her that he would establish the Carter Center, which would be a medium to settle international disputes. It was true that the UN was also created for a similar purpose, but he asked her what two nations would want to approach the UN with every other country interfering in their affairs. Instead, what he proposed was a smaller institution where the representatives could meet, away from the media glare and perhaps even in total secrecy. In Carter's own words, the purpose of the Carter Center is for "active" engagement with world problems. He did not create it to be a forum where scholars would debate and discuss issues. World problems would be studied only in order for concrete action to be taken.

Today, the Carter Center works to monitor electoral processes in countries to ensure that the establishment of democracy is a fair and transparent process. It conducts peace negotiations and talks between feuding peoples and also works around the globe to eradicate illnesses such as Guinea worm disease, filaria, and river blindness, among others. It also works in poorer African nations and elsewhere, specifically for women's and children's rights.

61: Conflict Resolution in North Korea

It was at President Clinton's behest that Carter undertook a visit to North Korea in 1994. The US was certain that the country was developing nuclear weapons on a large scale. The White House got wind of the fact that eight thousand rods of a nuclear reactor had been removed and suspected that the North Koreans might build bombs out of them. The then president of North Korea had also refused an international inspection of their plants, confirming the worst beliefs of the White House. The USA threatened North Korea with military action and cutting off trade relations.

However, the president of North Korea personally invited Carter to Pyongyang and the latter immediately set off to ease the political situation. Reminiscent of the Camp David days, Carter achieved what was touted to be impossible. A historic treaty was signed between North and South Korea after forty years of militancy. North Korea also agreed to stop its nuclear weapons expansion program.

62: Haiti

In 1994, President Clinton was poised to attack Haiti against those who had orchestrated an illegitimate political coup and ousted the democratic government. Even as Carter met with the leaders, US warships and planes were stationed to attack Haiti.

Clinton was clear that he would launch the attack despite the outcome of the talks. When the US forces reached Haitian soil, they realized that their mission was no longer the proposed attack on the rebel groups, but rather the peaceful task of transferring power back to the government authorities.

After deliberations with the leaders, Carter had been able to convince them to hand power back to the legitimate ruler peacefully. He thus averted what could have been a war accompanied by the loss of lives and property in Haiti.

63: The Fight Against Guinea Worm

In 1995, when a civil war was raging in Sudan, Jimmy Carter and Rosalynn went there as part of their crusade against the lethal Guinea worm disease. At the time, around a million people were dying annually of the disease, which often spreads via contaminated water and undercooked fish. The female of the species can grow as long as three feet and can leave painful open wounds on the legs and feet of the person infected, from where the worms emerge. Guinea worms can also spread from a contaminated person into bodies of water they come in contact with. The Carters were instrumental in a temporary ceasefire of the civil war for two months so that the affected people could be treated and the water sources in the villages could be purified.

There is a story behind what prompted Carter to take up arms against this particular disease. Carter's former drug control policy specialist, Peter Borne, was working on a UN initiative called the "Freshwater Decade." He was the one who introduced Carter to this often-overlooked problem because few other NGOs were coming forward to combat this despicable disease that affected some of the poorest and most obscure parts of Africa and Asia. For Carter, who loves a challenge, the rest was history.

Due to the relentless efforts of The Carter Center, Guinea worm disease stands to be the next disease that will be completely eradicated after smallpox. When Carter visited Sudan again in 2002 to participate in a Guinea worm awareness program sponsored by The Carter Center, UNICEF, WHO, and the Government of Sudan, he said that statistically, 98% of Guinea worms had already been eradicated, but that it would take the concerted effort of governments, health organizations, and the people to complete the mission. He has always maintained that his greatest wish is for the last Guinea worm to die before he does (Beaubien & Whitehead, 2023).

64: Building Homes for the Poor

The Carters have traveled to fourteen countries to build homes for the poor. His work with the Christian nonprofit organization Habitat for Humanity has provided thousands of people with affordable housing.

In 1984, a couple of months after he had started volunteering for Habitat, he was in New York on a speaking engagement. When he stopped by a Habitat working site, he promised them that he would return with more volunteers. Sticking to his word, he accompanied a busload of others from his church in Plains to New York and helped with the renovation of a six-story tenement building on East 6th Street. The incident was widely reported in the papers, with a headline in the *New York Times* that read, "Carpenter Named Carter Comes to New York."

Carter had always been interested in building things from wood and metal, even as a child. His native intelligence on the subject further fired up his humanitarian spirit in wanting to build homes for those who were too poor to afford them or those who had lost their homes in accidents or natural calamities. Every week for a year, the Carters would go personally to villages within and outside the US, roll up their sleeves, and get to work on the projects. It is estimated that the Carters have helped in building or repairing a total of 4,390 homes. Their effort, in turn, would invariably capture the attention of other builders and contractors who would join the mission.

Carter said of his work with Habitat that it was much more gratifying to work personally on such projects than the "pleasant" task of sitting in the office and signing bills that would appropriate funds or pass legislation for low-income housing projects in the country (Capps, 2023).

65: Emory University

Carter got several invitations to teach or take up academic positions at universities. He declined many of them but finally decided to become a "distinguished professor" at Emory University in 1982. He was to lecture college students and have full freedom of expression. Furthermore, he was exempted from grading papers and being involved with a specific class for a whole semester. His duties were more along the lines of providing guest lectures to various classes after having finalized the topics of discussion with teachers and deans. He also gave lectures every month in various schools and departments on a variety of subjects, including history, law, political science, business, environmental studies, African-American studies, medicine, and theology. He would often draw on his experience in office and as a businessman himself to speak to his students.

Every September, he would have to face a new class and would encourage them to ask questions. Some of these questions were both unpredictable and funny. There was, for instance, a debate on whether the ex-president liked his peanut butter smooth or crunchy. However, to date, Carter is proud of never having shied away from answering a question just because it touched a personal vein. He created media uproars with his frank comments on political and current issues.

Interestingly, the first office of The Carter Center was housed on the tenth floor of Emory University's Robert W. Woodruff Library, as The Carter Center building was being constructed. At the time, The Carter Center had only three staff including the ex-president himself.

66: Mental Health Awareness Campaign

For a very long time, even during Jimmy Carter's political life as a governor, Rosalynn had been involved in championing mental health awareness and campaigning for better facilities throughout the region and country to treat psychological illnesses. Her main idea was to try to remove the stigma associated with it because it halted progress. In fact, a little after Carter became the president, he set up the Presidential Commission on Mental Health to recommend policies and measures to bridge the gap in mental health care. This was a first of its kind and led to the completion of the National Plan for the Chronically Mentally Ill. However, owing to bureaucratic delays and other rivalries within the political system, a system of care and treatment for persons with serious mental illnesses was never created.

She continued her commitment to the cause even after the establishment of The Carter Center and headed programs related to mental health policies. The Carter Center helped in conducting and certifying courses for journalists so that they could report about mental health more accurately. The center was also instrumental in establishing governmental acts and policies for mental health services in countries such as Liberia.

Sadly, in May 2023, The Carter Center declared that Rosalynn was diagnosed with dementia.

Chapter 10:

Public Service and Civic Engagement

Carter has worn several hats throughout his life. From being a Navy man to a peanut farmer, a carpenter, and a president, there is no end to the number of things that he has been engaged in. Here, we try to find glimpses of the man engaged in things he loves best.

67: Author

As an author, Carter has written 33 books in all. The first one published was *Why Not the Best?* in 1975, which served as his campaign manifesto as well. As time progressed and he continued to maintain his journals, he loved the art of writing, which also served as a secondary source of income for the family. He also used most of his books to showcase his political views and ideology so that people could get to know him and his work at The Carter Center better.

In 1985, Carter published *The Blood of Abraham,* which covered his visits to the Middle Eastern countries of Jordan, Lebanon, Syria, Saudi Arabia, Israel, Palestine, and Egypt. He spoke to the key leaders of each of the places and maintained notes so that he could understand and write about what he felt would be a comprehensive peace strategy for the region.

Everything to Gain, coauthored by Jimmy and Rosalynn Carter, deals with the importance of physical health and how a person's commitment to habits can play a vital role in their overall health and longevity. The book saw acrimonious fights between the Carters when they initially tried to edit each other's work. There were also points of differences between how they saw things and the value they ascribed to certain subjects. They were almost on the brink of canceling the book and repaying the publisher's advance payment. However, the publisher came down to visit them in Plains, Georgia, and convinced them to continue and the paragraphs that created so much contention were marked with a "J" or an "R" to signify that it was their individual opinion.

An Outdoor Journal (1988) recounts Carter's experiences with and love for nature starting from when he was a boy to his travels in Alaska, Japan, and Nepal. *Turning Point* (1992) recounted Carter's first experience with dishonest voting practices and how he failed an election owing to it. There are also several books that serve as a testament to his faith in his God. Most of Carter's books have been international bestsellers.

There were a lot of other books, both political and apolitical, including a collection of poems he called *Always a Reckoning* (1995) that he penned, but one that stood out was *An Hour Before Daylight* (2002), which narrated in detail his experiences in Plains and his association with the Blacks of the community. It was a Pulitzer Prize finalist the same year.

68: Sunday School

Carter has never been one to shy away from his complete and total devotion to his faith and spreading the word via his missionary work. After his presidency, Carter continued to teach and speak vociferously about how his faith had been instrumental in shaping him. At the same time, he maintained that after his first defeat to Lester Maddox, he never suffered from either depression or a "mystical" call from God that instantly transformed his life. Instead, he prayed and he found that he felt closer to his maker. Clearly, he did not want his faith to be twisted into a public spectacle. One of the biggest aspects that Carter has continuously avowed is the separation of state and church. In other words, as a president, he would do what was best for the country, and as a Christian out of office, he would do what was best for his community and ministry. He never once invited Billy Graham or other pastors to the White House but instead continued worship on Sundays at a church of their choice.

When Carter took up Sunday school in Plains, the church was always packed to capacity, with 500 or more members coming to listen to him. His signature way to end his talk would be to ask his listeners to do one thing for another person over the coming month. Even as late as 2018, Carter used to stand at the podium for 45 minutes or slightly more to deliver his address. It was only afterward that he started using an electric lift chair. He stopped giving these lessons only with the onset of the pandemic and his own deteriorating health.

69: Agriculture

Carter met Nobel Laureate and agricultural expert Norman Borlaug and Japanese philanthropist Ryoichi Sasakawa in 1985, and they decided to work toward Global 2000 to increase the production of crops in African countries. The program was kickstarted in places such as Ghana, Zambia, Sudan, and Zimbabwe. It was expanded to 14 African nations. They were able to reach out to eight million African families and explain how to double or triple their production of rice, wheat, maize, sorghum, and millet.

With Japanese funding and the expertise of Borlaug, they were able to make quick progress by demonstrating the techniques to 40 farmers at a time. These farmers would then teach their neighbors to use the best seed, plant in such a way as to reduce erosion, use the right fertilizer, and farm and store their grains in the best manner possible. Carter kept traveling with Borlaug to meet with government officials and to ensure that these farming practices were followed by the farmers, too.

On one such trip to Ethiopia, Carter was staying in a hotel where he woke up to intense itching on one of his knees. On close inspection, he found two puncture marks there. He did not think much about it; he just applied some ointment and went back to sleep. By the next night, Carter's knee had swollen up. The doctor at the U.S. Embassy gave him some medicine and surmised that Carter had been bitten by a certain kind of spider. By then, the entire leg was swollen. Sensing a threat to Carter's life, the doctor had him flown to a military hospital in Germany. Once they realized the kind of spider that might have played a role in this episode, he had severe rashes all over his body and was taken back to Atlanta. Though Carter recovered, he still gets a rash at times, which has to be soothed with creams and medicated salves.

70: Carter Presidential Library and Museum

Since the time of Herbert Hoover, it has been customary for ex-presidents to use privately raised funds to establish a presidential library and museum in their names. As of today, 15 such libraries exist. The Carter Presidential Library was opened on October 1, 1986. It is home to 40 million pages of written material, 40,000 artifacts, 2,500 hours of audio and video tapes, and 500,000 photos.

Carter had to raise $25 million in funds from friends and donors to build this library. In fact, after the Carter Center was completed, the first five years of its mission were to raise the requisite amount to complete the construction of the library and its museum in Atlanta.

Today, the library is partly held and run by the government, while some sections are privately held and run by the Carters.

There are many presidents who chose to be buried in their respective presidential libraries after their deaths. However, Carter has expressly wished to be interred in Plains. The Carters have planned for their house to be converted into a museum after their lives end.

To think that Carter was so full of energy to do so much even after the stress and pressure of the president's office is just remarkable. One of the biggest factors that helped him achieve all that he has achieved today has been the unwavering support of his close-knit family. We will look at his relationship with them next.

Chapter 11:

Family and Legacy

Jimmy Carter was the eldest of his parents' four children. As a young boy, Jimmy was impressed with his father's hard work around the farm and used to idolize him. His mother, being a nurse, was often absent from Jimmy's home life because she used to spend long hours at the hospital where she worked as a nurse. It wasn't exactly a traditional home that he grew up in. For instance, Jimmy would remember his father cooking more meals for the children than his mother did. Later in life, he would realize the significance of his mother's work and how it contributed to their family budget, as well as her ideology and its impact on him.

71: Mama

Bessie Lilly Gordy, Jimmy's mother, was born in Richland. She worked in the postal department before shifting to Plains to complete a training course as a nurse and also to work at the Wise Sanitarium there. Her family did not approve of her choice of career. However, she was determined and became successful at her work. She was popular among both the Whites and Blacks of her community, who lovingly called her "Miss Lillian."

Lillian Gordy wasn't exactly a religious woman and when her family attended service at church on Sundays, she conducted her own Bible study at home. After the death of Earl Carter, Lillian served as housemother of the Kappa Alpha Order, which catered to a hundred boys at Auburn University. Then, she went on to manage a nursing home in Blakely afterward. She also worked as an anti-segregationist in

Plains. At the age of 68, she worked as a peace volunteer in India, even working with leprosy patients for nearly two years.

There are a couple of interesting anecdotes about her. When Carter told his mother that he was running to become the president, she asked him, "President of what?" When he clarified, she only told him to get his legs off her quilt. This laconic reply was characteristic of Lillian.

Another incident that involved her was when Carter was campaigning to become president. With her characteristic Southern hospitality, she welcomed the press who had come to interview her, remarking how nice it was to see them, whether they wanted a glass of lemonade, and so on. When a reporter asked her whether it was true that Jimmy Carter never lied, she answered that he said white lies all the time. The reporter wanted to know what she meant by a *white* lie and she responded wittily by saying that her saying it was nice to see them earlier was an instance of a white lie.

Lillian was, in her day, as independent and bold as a woman can be and that resilience of spirit was inherited by her son as well. During Jimmy Carter's presidency, his mother published two books, both released in 1977: *Miss Lillian and Friends* and *Away from Home: Letters to my Family*.

72: Daddy

Jimmy Carter's father, Earl Carter, was a stern disciplinarian. With Jimmy being his firstborn, he had big aspirations for him. Of course, if he could have seen Carter when he became the president, he might have admitted that Jimmy lived up to or perhaps even outlived them all. As it stood, Jimmy had a hard time pleasing his father. Jimmy has claimed how it was hard to get a word of praise from Earl Carter.

Jimmy Carter has himself remarked that he nearly *worshiped* his father, who was the dominant member of their family and in Jimmy's life. When we look at how Earl Carter built up his life in an era of poverty, it is not hard to see why Jimmy was so in awe of him. Earl Carter helped his children get to school, arranged their lunchboxes, and even helped them with their homework. Clearly, it was the part that was to have been traditionally played by the mother of the house and yet Earl did it without any complaint. However, he was also demanding in his expectations of them and would give them chores that they had to complete. Jimmy Carter would remember him as a man who showed his children little affection outwardly, even though he was a thoroughly responsible parent when it came to their needs.

Earl Carter bought Jimmy his first air gun, but also told him to shoot responsibly, only that which he intended to eat. One day, Jimmy shot a quail and ran home excitedly to show the bird to his father. His father asked him where his gun was. A deflated Jimmy realized belatedly that he had dropped his gun in the bushes and forgotten all about it in his excitement. In fact, years later, in the only poem that Jimmy Carter ever wrote about his dad, he penned lines about the pain he still felt at not having received a paternal hug or word of praise.

73: Rosalynn

Ironically enough, Rosalynn Smith was delivered by Lillian Carter in the home of the Smiths in 1927. A 3-year-old Jimmy saw her through the bars of her cradle on the same day. That she should become Jimmy's wife seemed to be almost written in the stars. Rosalynn was Jimmy's sister Ruth's best friend who was always welcome at the Carter home. Earl Carter was very fond of Rosalynn and it was only a matter of time before she captured Jimmy's attention and heart.

On Jimmy's graduation from the Naval Academy, he let both his mother and his sweetheart pin the ensign badges on him, a role usually reserved for one "special woman" in the navy man's life. You could clearly see the love he bore the two women who played such big roles in his life.

If there ever was a couple who could swear to have had an equal partnership in life, that would be Jimmy and Rosalynn. Most political aides of the time knew that if there was anyone who could change the president's mind it was only his wife, who was sometimes referred to as the "steel magnolia," owing to her disciplined lifestyle. She was well-versed in the political work of her husband and represented him in several meetings with diplomats. She was the goodwill ambassador to the Latin American countries. She ran her own campaigns for mental health advocacy, the rights of women and children, and giving support to both professional and family caregivers. She was known for her practical frugality, whether it was the menus for her guests or even her own dresses. She wore the same gown for the presidential inaugural ball as she had for the governor's ball when her husband had been elected in Georgia.

She was also an author in her own right, having published five books after her husband's presidency. One of these was her autobiography, one a self-help book on making the most of one's life co-authored with Jimmy Carter, another on the responsibilities of a caregiver, and two books on mental health issues.

In 2023, around the time when Jimmy Carter entered hospice care at home, Rosalynn was diagnosed with dementia. People close to them reveal how the couple still hold hands after 77 years of marriage. Until a few years ago, they used to read the Bible together every day and try to improve their Spanish by reading books to each other.

74: Gloria

Gloria, one of Jimmy's sisters, was the closest to him in age, being born only two years after he was. She was nicknamed "GoGo" by her dad. As a girl, she was often with her mother or the nanny who took care of them, involved in tasks in and around the house, just as Jimmy was always milling around his father, pressing him for more information on how the farm worked. Physically bigger than Jimmy, she used to get the better of him, early on in their tiffs. As time went on, however, Jimmy got busy with the other boys around the farm and he actively ignored her. Even when Gloria joined him at school, Jimmy was ashamed of her because he thought she was not sophisticated enough and too "country." A primary reason for this was that Gloria had only picked up the Black dialect of English and spoke like the Blacks with whom they had grown up. An incident verified by Jimmy Carter was how she threw a wrench at him on one occasion. Unthinkingly, he shot her with his BB gun in retaliation, for which he was whipped soundly by their father.

Gloria was sort of the "wild child" in the family and the only one who had enough courage to oppose their father. She received more spankings from Earl Carter than Jimmy ever did. Adventurous as she was, she initially enrolled in the Cadet Nurse Corps in Maryland. She married and moved to Texas a little later, a union that her parents had not approved of. The marriage eventually fell through and Gloria returned to Plains and remarried. However, she wrote poems, painted, and became a motorcyclist and a den mother to motorbike groups.

She was a great help to Jimmy Carter during his gubernatorial campaigning in his hometown. She handled the accounts, sent articles to newspapers, responded to invitations for speaking, and sent letters to Jimmy and Rosalynn in Atlanta sharing all the news. The campaign headquarters in Plains was her domain. However, once Jimmy became the president, Gloria and her husband shied away from media publicity. She chose to focus on her Harley-Davidson motorcycling trips. She was one of the first women in the Harley-Davidson 100,000 Mile Club.

75: Ruth

Ruth, another of his sisters, was five years younger than Jimmy. Chubby, blonde, and pretty even as a baby, she was the apple of Earl's eyes. In fact, her father used to take her along for many of his public events rather than his wife. He used to remark that Ruth was prettier than Shirley Temple, the cherubic Hollywood baby star.

Ruth and Jimmy never interacted much as children, most probably owing to the age gap and Jimmy's early induction into the Navy. Like her brother, Ruth was good at her studies and went on to complete her bachelor's degree in English and master's in psychology. She did not have an easy life. For much of her life, she was depressed and could not attend to the needs of her family, which had grown to include four children. There are speculations that her depression began after her father's death in 1953.

She eventually turned to religion and underwent intense psychotherapy, after which she could lead a fuller and more functional life. She was instrumental to a large extent in various facets of Jimmy's life. If not for her intervention, Jimmy and Rosalynn might not have ended up married.

Much later, when Carter lost the first elections for the Georgia governor's office, it was a walk in the woods with Ruth that helped Jimmy realize his purpose, and also find God in his life. He would speak of his experience as being "born again."

In her lifetime, Ruth Carter Stapleton published six books, all related to faith and finding healing through spiritual experiences.

76: Billy

Thirteen years younger than Jimmy, his brother Billy Carter was the youngest sibling and the baby of the house. He was Jimmy's managing partner when the latter returned to Plains to oversee the large estates left to the family by Earl Carter. An industrialist and agriculturist at heart, Billy promoted a variant of the peanut crop—peanut Lolita and his brew, which he called Billy Beer. His political forays weren't very successful, and though he tried for Governorship in Plains, he never won. In the 1970s, he bought a gas station in Plains, which yielded his family huge profits over a decade.

Jimmy's political opponents often used Billy to humiliate him. Billy was eccentric and once even went as far as to urinate on the airport runway in plain sight of the press. A rather embarrassing incident was when Billy and a Georgia group traveled to Libya to borrow a sum of $220,000 from the government there. Jimmy Carter had to give his reassurance to the public that Billy's actions would never influence U.S. policy or actions with regard to Libya. Though nobody knows for sure, this loan, except for a token amount of $1,000, was never repaid by

Billy. This episode was often referred to as the Billygate scandal, after the infamous Watergate.

Billy became an alcoholic and recovered from addiction. Later in life, he turned to supporting other addicts, helping them to overcome their problems. Like Earl Carter, Ruth, and Gloria, Billy too died of pancreatic cancer, at the age of 51.

77: Amy

Born in 1967, Amy was only 9 years old when her father became the president of the US. Staying at the White House for her was a grander version of her stay at the Georgia governor's house. She was one of the few children to have lived in the White House since President Kennedy's time. Thus, she got a lot of media attention. It must have been an unconventional life for a little girl.

She spent her time roller skating in the East Room, and in the tree house her father built for her in the South Lawn. When her friends came visiting, she had security agents monitoring the group the whole time. She attended public school in Washington, D.C., because the Carters did not think it was right for her to go to a swanky private one.

When Amy was asked by reporters whether she had anything to tell other children of America, she thought about it seriously for a while before saying "No."

When Jimmy won the election for the governor's office, he held up Amy, who was a toddler at the time, for the crowds to see. Much later, in his election debate against Reagan, he would tell the world that he asked his daughter about what she thought was the most important problem in the world, and that she said it was the control of nuclear arms.

Some of the Carter charm that worked its magic on the public, especially during the early Carter era, was definitely owing to Amy.

Whether Amy talked of nuclear arms or not, she later espoused some of her dad's zeal in fighting for human rights, especially against apartheid in South Africa. She was part of several student protests at the university where she was studying and even got arrested more than once for it.

Chapter 12:

Friendship, Alliances, and Influences

Throughout his life, there were people of all different races who greatly influenced Jimmy Carter apart from his parents. We look at some of these people who had a major role in shaping the beloved president's life and views.

78: A.D.

Alonzo David, who was called A.D. by everyone, was Jimmy's best friend when he grew up in Plains. He lived with his uncle and aunt on Jimmy's farmland. Initially, Jimmy, who had seen and played only with White boys up until then, was quite intrigued by A.D.'s Black skin, large eyes, and kinky hair. A.D. was very shy and mumbled around the Whites. But Jimmy noticed that when adults were not around, A.D. quickly found his voice. They spent their days playing, fishing, crafting things, and swimming in the lakes and around the farmlands. His aunt and uncle never quite knew A.D.'s actual date of birth, but they adopted Jimmy's birthdate as A.D.'s so that the two boys could celebrate the day together. When they were young, the boys hardly seemed to notice the racial divide between them. Each of them was comfortable in the other's house. When there was not much work in the fields, Earl Carter would let Jimmy and A.D. travel to Americus to watch a movie, where they would have to be seated separately as per the segregation rules of the time. When they had to go back, they would be briefly united in their walk before again being separated on the bus.

Much later, A.D. was accused of killing an employer in self-defense. Though Jimmy Carter never acknowledged this, he helped A.D. get the lesser sentence of manslaughter and used his influence as the governor to have him released in 18 months. In his autobiography, Carter only mentions how A.D. was convicted on a forgery case, though in reality, there never was such a registered case against him. A.D. went on to marry and establish his long line of descendants in Plains.

Possibly because of his close interaction with the Blacks, Jimmy learned to speak both the White and Black dialects of English, which were very different not just in vocabulary, grammar, and sentence structure, but also in the rhythm and speech patterns.

79: Rembert

Rembert Forrest was the only other White boy in Jimmy's group of friends. He was the eldest foster son of Mr. Forrest, who ran a large sawmill in Plains. Mrs. Forrest had died and the boy had only his adoptive father. When Rembert became dangerously ill and it was feared he would die, Mr. Forrest hired Jimmy's mother to care for the boy 24/7. Thus, Lillian became more of a mother than a nurse to Rembert. As he started recovering, Lillian would bring the boy home more often to stay with her family. This was how Jimmy's friendship with him began.

Jimmy was often envious of how Rembert's father got him a Shetland pony after he recovered. They would often go riding it together. The pony, being a habitually nervous creature, would startle easily and throw the boys off its back.

Jimmy remembers how well he got along with Rembert and A.D., despite their various eccentricities. For instance, every time a camera was produced, Rembert would hurry to comb his hair and make himself presentable, while A.D. often refused to get photographed because he had heard that photos took something out of one's body.

Eventually, Rembert became a successful funeral director, and he and his family moved to Florida after his retirement.

80: Annie Mae

Annie Mae Hollis was a Black woman who was employed by the Carter household as a nanny and housekeeper to the children, as Lillian Carter tended to her patients. She was a favorite with all of them and was exceptionally close to Gloria and Ruth. She stayed with the family. Carter tells of how Black women shaped him throughout his childhood, and how he came to regard them as almost mother figures. She later moved on to work with a couple in Hollywood.

So strong was Annie Mae's devotion to the Carter family that she returned when she heard that Earl Carter was terminally ill. In fact, he breathed his last in her arms, while Jimmy watched on in the room. She never flinched, even when covered with his black vomit.

Several years later, when Annie Mae's home in Albany was destroyed by a flood, it was Jimmy and Rosalynn's pleasure to restore it for her as part of their volunteering for Habitat for Humanity.

81: Rachel Clark

Rachel Clark, the wife of Jack Clark, was one of the biggest influences on Jimmy's early life. She used to take him fishing often and care for him occasionally like a nanny. He admits that after his parents, she was the one with whom he was closest. He often worked with her in the fields, trying to keep up with her pace and dexterity. He also used to spend time at their residence, and on colder nights, she would move his cot closer to the only fire in their small hut. It was a neat, clean place where Jimmy could go, especially when his parents were away.

The Clarks loved Jimmy like a son, and through them, he was able to witness the poverty and frustrations of the Blacks and yet how they maintained their dignity and faith through all the troubles.

Rachel Carter was too dignified to play with the Carter children. Yet, they respected her calm sense of dignity. Though illiterate, she had an innate sense of wisdom, which she passed on to her wards. Carter's lifelong love for nature was probably instilled in him by Rachel Clark, as she used to give him small lectures about nature and God.

Much later, when she was interviewed, Rachel Clark remembered the Carter children as well-behaved. She was especially fond of Jimmy, who was quiet, with his love for reading and his faith. This was why she did not mind having him home often and following her about trying to help her with her chores.

Jimmy Carter must have prized her among the few people he loved most, for among the poems he wrote to his mother, father, and Rosalynn, there was one that he wrote for Rachel Clark.

82: Julia Coleman

Julia Coleman was the teacher that Jimmy Carter quoted in his inaugural address as the president. He said that she taught him how "you must accommodate changing times but cling to unchanging principles" (Carter, 2016, p. 67). She was fond of the bright, quiet boy in her class who loved to read. So great was his love, in fact, that she even used to borrow additional books for him from the county library. She encouraged Jimmy to read by suggesting books and ensuring that the library was well-stocked. Thus, Jimmy read books that were way beyond the level of the class he was in, often preferring classics. She also developed in Jimmy a taste for classical music and art. Under her guidance, the class would put on plays and read from the Bible.

Julia Coleman, who was the daughter of a Baptist minister, never married but was instead devoted to her school and its work. She bore a limp from an early injury and was almost blind in one eye, owing to retinal bleeding. Though there were several students who remembered her with fondness, Jimmy held a special place in his heart for her.

At the time she taught his class, Julia Coleman had been to the White House and even met with First Lady Eleanor Roosevelt, at the latter's invitation. She used to occasionally correspond with Mrs. Roosevelt. Little would the teacher imagine that one day, a little boy in her class would not only grow up to become the president but also remember her in his inaugural speech. Though she had lived long enough to see Jimmy Carter become the governor, she passed on by the time he was sworn in as president.

83: Admiral Rickover

Hyman Rickover greatly influenced Jimmy Carter's work ethic. Like Jimmy's father, Rickover was a perfectionist who hardly ever showered praise on anybody, even if their work deserved it. In fact, if you look at it, both Rickover and Carter, though separated by more than two decades in age, were similar. They were extremely patriotic but misunderstood in their time. Rickover's report on Jimmy was filled with praises for his excellent administrative and leadership role on board the U.S.S. *Seawolf*. In turn, when Jimmy Carter published his first book, *Why Not the Best?* in 1975, just before the presidential elections, the title was a tribute to Rickover's question to him in 1952 during his interview for the select program.

You would think that with Jimmy Carter's resignation from the Navy, he would have no more opportunity to associate with the formidable but extremely clever Admiral Hyman Rickover, who was almost disdainful of Carter's decision to quit. Thus, it was with a lot of pleasure that President Carter reestablished ties with the latter. He was open with Carter and told him at the outset that he wouldn't pester the president with budget allocations or priorities for any naval ship.

He was the one who advised Carter that breeder reactors were unnecessary at the time because they consumed more power than they produced. Thus, the initial plan to generate electricity from a chain of breeder reactors was scrapped. As usual, the decision was met with a lot of opposition in Congress, where most preferred to go ahead with the program that had been put in place by President Nixon. The cost of this project was initially estimated at $400 million but had increased to $3.2 billion by the time Carter decided to cancel it. More than the cost itself, Carter worried about the large quantities of the by-product, plutonium, that the plant would produce, which could be used by unscrupulous elements to cause nuclear explosions. Rickover concurred with Carter that the total elimination of nuclear weapons from the face of the earth would be a great achievement indeed.

Apart from the amazing people who helped Jimmy Carter on his quest to do the best by the people he led, one important factor helped him remain positive throughout his life: his faith. Let us look at what made Carter different from the other leaders of his time.

Chapter 13:

Faith and Optimism

84: The Essay on Faith

In a not-so-well-known essay that Jimmy wrote for his class when he was around 12, he talks of the habits that have a good effect on your health. He says thinking the right way will help one "develop (Ariail & Heckler-Feltz, 1996)

1. The habit of expecting to accomplish what you attempt.

2. The habit of expecting to like other people and to have them like you.

3. The habit of deciding quickly what you want to do and doing it quickly.

4. The habit of "sticking to it."

5. The habit of welcoming fearlessly all wholesome ideas and experiences.

6. A person who wants to build good mental habits should avoid idle daydreams, should give up worry and anger, hatred and envy, and should neither fear nor be ashamed of anything that is honest or purposeful" (p. 33).

This early essay is indicative of the great faith that Carter had in the power of the mind to achieve what it sets out to do if one is disciplined. This essay also shows how, from an early age, Jimmy Carter believed that if you thought right, you could make a difference in the world.

85: Inspiring Faith

There are smaller victories that Carter gained that are not well known today. For instance, when he traveled to North Korea in 1994, to talk to the president about standing down the latter's weaponization program, there was another incident for which he never got any credit. During the Korean conflict, about 5,000 Americans were buried in Korean cemeteries. These burials were done by American soldiers for their comrades and so the locations of these graves were well-known. Carter wanted to recover the remains of the soldiers so that they could be returned to their families back in America.

Initially, the North Korean president was dismissive of the idea. He wanted to defer discussions about it for another time. But Carter insisted, so much so that an argument broke out among officials. Everyone, including Carter, kept looking at what had happened. Finally, it was the North Korean president's wife who took control of the situation and said just three words in English, which led to the accomplishment of what Carter wanted. She said, "Just do it!"

And just like that, because of the honesty and trust he exuded, Jimmy Carter was not just able to defuse the volatility between America and North Korea but also managed to bring home the remains of the war heroes who had lost their lives in North Korea.

86: Spiritual Fitness

During the campaigning leading up to the presidential elections in 1976, a reporter casually asked Carter how he managed to keep himself mentally and spiritually fit. Carter said that he did not require special effort for this and that it was innately part of his nature. He mentioned how he read a chapter out of the Bible in Spanish every day and unfailingly kept a brief worship time set aside for God daily. These were the two practices that helped him remain strong.

He said at that time, every day, almost as unconscious as breathing, he would say a prayer or meditate, not in a structured fashion, but simply asking his maker to grant him wisdom or understanding of the troubles of the people.

The incident reminds us why Carter stood out in times of dwindling faith.

87: Practicing What He Preached

If Jimmy Carter preached about having faith in the innate goodness of mankind, those weren't empty words. He always matched his actions to his beliefs. Mary Prince, a Black American woman, was charged with manslaughter and was serving her sentence when the Carters met her in 1971. It was later proven that the charges were false. The mother of three was framed for a murder she did not commit. As she was poor and Black, she couldn't afford to contest the verdict.

Owing to her exemplary record, she was sent to the governor's house as a nanny. It was a standing practice for prisoners to be used for service in the homes of government officials. It was thus that Amy Carter took a liking to her. So strong was their bond, in fact, that Amy would feign illness if Mary did not come for a while. As for Mary, it had been a long while since she had felt loved or appreciated by anyone.

Prince attributes her gaining of faith to the Carters. At a time when she had stopped going to church, they invited her to mass. After a lot of soul searching, she felt like renewing her faith and finally, got baptized.

What really touched her was the fact that the Carters accepted her like family despite her having spent time in jail. As the governor, Carter had the case investigated thoroughly and when it came to light that she was innocent, he initiated the pardon against her. She was released and became a full-time nanny to Amy. She says that they never introduced her as a nursemaid or nanny; instead, they would always describe her as a good friend of the family.

88: The Malaise Speech

Carter's televised speech from July 1979 was iconically labeled the "malaise" speech, even though he never once used that word in the entirety of a slightly more than half-an-hour-long speech. The speech garnered attention in the wake of the growing discontent with Carter's government and its inability to curb inflation, oil prices, and the growing unemployment. Though reviews of the address were mixed to negative at the time, today, we remember it as a historical moment for America.

Carter does not shy away from addressing the frustrations, despair, and troubles that America was going through just then. However, he also asks for faith from the people in the American institutions and government. He believed that change could stem only from faith. He then goes on to address what he believed was the biggest problem that the Americans were facing—the energy crisis. In six points, he sums up what the course of action would be.

Firstly, he said that the country would focus on the production of oil and energy within its shores so that it wouldn't be dependent on foreign oil. Secondly, he said that he would use his presidential authority to curb oil imports into the country starting immediately. Thirdly, he pledged American funds for the development of alternative sources of energy from sun, shale, and unconventional gas. Next, he said that he would mandate Congress to cut down the consumption of oil by large companies by 50% and for them to switch to other sources of energy. Fifthly, he promised quick implementation of energy-related bills without red tape and procedural delays. Lastly, he proposed a bold conservation strategy in which organizations, governments, and even citizens could contribute by implementing energy-saving methods at home.

The speech is a testament to Carter's firm faith in the fact that people can change things if they believe they can. He knew that it was possible because that was how he had led his own life. If he believed he could do it, he simply did it.

Rooted in faith as he was, Carter was also dynamic when it came to the adoption of various skills and artistic pursuits. In the next chapter, we look at all the ways in which Carter was a complete man.

Chapter 14:

Embracing Change and Evolution

Jimmy Carter was not just an entrepreneur or a politician. He was a man who took immense pride in being good at the many things he dabbled in. It is evident that he took a keen pleasure in life itself. Let us look at a few things that he loves doing even to this day.

89: Rock N' Roll President

Interestingly, you will find among Jimmy Carter's memorabilia in the Carter Presidential Museum, a report card of his from the sixth standard in which he has an A grade in every subject, but music, for which alone he has been marked down with a B.

Jimmy Carter is usually thought of as a mild-mannered president, wanting to do good, but cautious about each step he takes. He is not the one you would think to label as the Rock and Roll President. However, a 2020 documentary titled exactly that showcased Carter as the ultimate lover of music—whether it is devotional songs, classical music, or the rebellious rock and roll culture that was popularized by the likes of Johnny Cash and Elvis Presley. In fact, the documentary tells us how Carter was able to tap into his love for music and, thus, forge a closer relationship with the common man.

He has Ms. Julia Coleman to thank for his introduction to and love for classical music, which was further strengthened by his roommate at Georgia Tech, Robert Ormsby, who had a fine collection of records that they used to listen to. At Annapolis, Carter was delighted to make the acquaintance of Robert Scott, a concert pianist. In fact, Carter tells us in his memoirs how they used to spend their monthly allowance on buying records of classical compositions (Carter, 2016, p. 28). In fact, during his interview, Rickover had asked him about his taste in music, to which Carter had honestly replied that he leaned toward country and jazz music, though he knew more about classical. Rickover asked still more specific questions on classical music, all of which Carter was able to answer.

Jimmy Carter was on excellent terms with musicians like Elvis Presley, Bono, the Allman Brothers, and Bob Dylan—a fact that not everyone knows. In fact, as early as his stint as the governor, Carter took pains to strengthen copyright laws for singers and musicians so that they wouldn't suffer heavy losses from piracy.

People who did not know Carter well often thought that his public appearances with music bands were publicity stunts aimed at garnering him the support of the younger generation. However, the fact was Carter thoroughly enjoyed music.

90: Carpentry

There must have been a reason that Jimmy Carter's going away present from the White House staff was an order to Sears for power tools that would enable the ex-president to build furniture. People who knew Carter also knew of his great love for making things out of wood.

From a young age, Carter loved working with wood and crafting useful things out of it—furniture, souvenir pieces, and many other things. In fact, when the Carters returned to Plains after Carter's naval career, it was he who made the furniture for their government house on lease. In the four years that the Carters were in the White House, their small house back in Plains had fallen to disrepair. He took great joy in getting a log cabin built near Turniptown Creek. He designed and built chairs, tables, beds, storage cabinets, and other furniture for this second house. He also studied Colonial carpentry techniques that would enable him to craft furniture without the use of nails and glue.

Until very recently, Carter used to make furniture which would then be auctioned at the Carter Center and the proceeds would be used for various causes.

91: Writing and Poetry

Carter had a lifelong love for writing. From the moment he was enrolled in school, Carter could be found with his nose in a book when not working. It is this enormous love of reading that made him the writer he is today. We did discuss many of his books written during and after his presidency.

The fact that he never stuck to specific genres like some of the more academically inclined writers can be seen from the fact that his complete bibliography includes even a children's book, *The Little Baby Snoogle-Fleejer* (1995), which was illustrated by his daughter, Amy.

He wrote a book of poems, *Always a Reckoning* (1994), in which he talks of his relationship with people, places, and events that influenced his life. Jimmy Carter remains the only president in US history to have a book of poems published in his name.

He also wrote a novel, *The Hornet's Nest,* in 2003, which is a historical fictional story set in 1766 around the Civil War era, for which he did extensive research.

Jimmy Carter's talents in diverse areas never cease to amaze.

92: Winemaking

The Carters were into winemaking even before Jimmy's time. His grandfather had 15 acres of vineyard from where they used to source grapes for wine. Both Earl and Billy Carter were winemakers who handed down their recipe to Jimmy. Jimmy started concocting and perfecting his blend in the 1990s. It wasn't a primary trade, but every five years or so, he would produce about a hundred bottles of red and white wine put together. He has donated several of these bottles to the Carter Center. In an interview, he tells us how he dramatically changed the recipe of his wine to suit the modern palate, which currently goes light on sugar intake (Isaac, 2005).

When asked about how he goes about the process, Carter says that he follows books on it and internet recipes, while also getting the equipment and advice from a store in Atlanta that specializes in everything related to winemaking. He also describes how he has a 250-year-old wine press that someone gave him and other equipment that he made himself.

Incidentally, Jimmy Carter was a president who broke the precedent of serving hard liquor in the White House. He estimated that $1 million a year was saved in this manner. However, when president, they still continued to serve good wine to the guests, which was domestically brewed in the country.

93: Hunting and Fishing

It was Rachel Clark who taught Jimmy fishing, and since then, he has been fond of fishing in the creeks around his farmlands. He and his friends would mostly catch catfish and eels, which they cooked and ate. In fact, sometimes, the boys would hold competitions as to who could catch the greatest number of fish.

He also often went hunting with his father or one of the farmhands. They caught raccoons, opossums, and quails. Jimmy's first BB gun was a gift from his father. Earl's only injunction to his son was to hunt responsibly, or in other words, only to feed his hunger.

Carter continued his tradition of hunting and fishing at Camp David or elsewhere when he was the president. A lover of the outdoors, it is claimed that he spent nearly all his vacation days hunting or fishing. In 2019, he was about to go on a turkey hunt, when he fell and broke his hips. He needed to undergo hip replacement surgery. When asked about his injury, the former president was more concerned that he would miss the turkey season, which ended soon, and that he would have to wait a whole year to go turkey hunting again. He also hoped that the state of Georgia would allow him to roll over his unused limit that year for the next.

The incident not only highlights Carter's love for hunting but also his keen sense of humor, even when faced with difficulties.

94: Painting

In addition to being everything that he was, Jimmy Carter is a painter of considerable skill. As with his woodwork, which he uses to raise money for charitable causes, he has his paintings auctioned at the Carter Center for similar purposes. Oil painting wasn't a gift Jimmy noticed in himself when he was young; rather, it was something he took up in his spare time. He has produced over a hundred pieces, mostly portraying people, places, and life in his beloved hometown and a few about his travels abroad. Some of his notable works have been included in his autobiography, *A Full Life: Reflections at 90,* published in 2015.

95: Environmentalism

He may perhaps not have called himself that, but Carter was definitely one of the finest environmentalist politicians of his time. Apart from the Alaskan reserves that he helped create, he also opened up a superfund to evacuate and resettle 800 families near Love Canal in the city of Niagara Falls, New York, who were living on top of a toxic waste landfill. A containment area was created for the waste so that it wouldn't affect people living around it. This was the first time that a fund had been created for such a purpose.

We have talked already about Carter's prescient vision about how fossil fuels would deplete over time and how America ought to embrace other sources of energy. In fact, Carter appointed Gustave Speth to the President's Council on Environmental Quality, a move that surprised many, because Speth was an unapologetic radical when it came to environmental conservation.

Under Speth, Carter learned more about "acid rain, carbon dioxide buildup in the atmosphere, and the likely extinction of 100,000 species during the next quarter century." (Bird, 2023). Carter was also one of the first presidents to talk about the increased use of solar energy. He went on to install solar panels on the White House, which were unfortunately torn down by the next president, Ronald Reagan.

Carter was also against the creation of too many dams in the country, as he rightly gauged that it would cause havoc with the natural flow of the rivers, creating floods in some areas and drought in others. Apart from the environmental factors, there was also the wastage of funds and the money certain congressmen surreptitiously made from it, every time such a project was approved. As governor and later as president, Carter ensured that each of these proposed water projects got his full attention before they were approved so that the costs of building these dams wouldn't exceed the benefits they gave the public.

Before Carter's term ended, he wrote up a report that talked about global climatic changes and the dangers that it posed if humankind persisted in its use of fossil fuels. The report has been eerily prophetic.

Above everything else, Carter's life has been a true testament to the ability of what man can achieve if he has the mind and will to do it.

Chapter 15:

A Life of Service and Purpose

Jimmy Carter was once troubled by a question he had heard: "If you were on trial for being a Christian, would there be enough evidence to convict you?" Carter says that this question opened up all the guilt he felt at being more of a politician than a man who was working the will of his God. Even his political ambitions were colored by the good he could do for the people around him. In this last section, we examine why Jimmy Carter's life has been one of service and purpose.

96: "Don't Get Weary, Don't Be Afraid, Don't Give Up."

Tony Lowden, who was the pastor of Maranatha Baptist Church, where the Carters worshiped, and a close friend of Jimmy Carter, still visits him in his Plains home, where he is presently in hospice care. When Lowden asked him for a message, what Carter told him sums up the ex-president's take on life and his home country. He said, "Don't get weary, don't Be afraid, don't give up, because this is a great nation" (CBS News, 2023a).

Lowden tells us how he has never met anyone quite like Jimmy Carter—"not even close," he says, trying to explain how special Carter is (CBS News, 2023a). Lowden recalled a trip they made to a Black cemetery in Plains, where thousands of men who gave up their lives for Georgia were buried. Lowden recalls how, on a hot morning, the ex-president, enfeebled with age, and in a wheelchair being pushed by his aides, pointed out the grave of Bishop William Decker Johnson and described him as the AME Bishop who introduced Carter to Christ. Lowden tells us how people who understand the impact of racism are today termed "woke," but that Jimmy Carter was aware so many years ago.

Lowden said that when he prayed with Carter, the latter still prayed for others around him. He had only one way of describing Carter: "A servant's leader with a servant's heart."

97: "A Life Very Well Done"

In a small trading post store in Plains, which stocks all the political memorabilia associated with not just Carter but the whole of the US, storekeeper Philip Kurland, who runs the store with his wife, is incredibly proud of the honor that Carter did them by visiting his store often. He was happy that people like the Carters should care about them. The store stocks pins and posters from Carter's campaigns, the Annapolis student yearbook entry on Carter, mugs, hats, stickers, books, and a wide variety of things that justifiably remind Plains of why it should be proud of Carter.

Carter was one of Kurland's most frequent customers. He says of the Carters that they are the most down-to-earth people he has met. He recounts a funny incident when Rosalynn Carter wanted to buy some souvenirs from him for five dollars and Jimmy Carter hollered, "Five dollars?" incredulous that she would want to spend so much. If Carter was a president who endorsed frugality, he still seems to swear by it.

Kurland also described a time when he had been hospitalized and how Carter had come and sat with him for an hour.

When asked what he would write on a button today in tribute to Carter's life, Kurland said without hesitation, "A life very well done" (CBS News, 2023b).

98: A Full Life

In 1994, when Carter was 70, a ceremony was organized in the state capitol in Atlanta, where a slightly larger-than-life statue of his was being unveiled. The statue depicted Carter in "working man" attire of khaki pants, and a shirt with sleeves rolled up. The sculptor Frederick Hart deliberately did not depict the famous toothy Carter grin, which had been caricatured by the press and cartoonists endlessly.

A small crowd who adored their local ex-president stood listening to a series of speeches, impatiently waiting to hear Carter's words. When it was Carter's chance to speak, he said that he was both grateful and embarrassed by all the recognition showered on him, that was reserved for most leaders posthumously. He then went on to elaborate on a theme that he has often spoken about. He said that his work as president had receded to the past and that he was gladder about the "full life" he had been able to lead as a Georgian and a Southerner.

On that day, an onlooker, Cecil Randolph, reached out to touch the outstretched arm of Carter's statue and said that Carter had helped so many people and that he simply had to touch him (Morris, 1996).

99: Shining Ex-President

Unlike the armchair politics endorsed by many politicians after their term in office, Carter was out there with his power tools building and repairing homes, using his political acumen to advise and help his successors, or going abroad to negotiate peace between fighting regions. He did not choose to just sit in an air-conditioned room, pulling strings to get things done. Instead, he took on the mantle of responsibility personally, went out and made a difference to people out there. His work wasn't glamorous, but he got up and did it anyway.

The *Los Angeles Times* once said of Carter that in addition to the book-writing and sulking that characterized the lives of most presidents,

Carter was still working hard on achieving what eluded him in office. Quoting from the Bible, the press called him a "prophet without honor in his own land, which was a shame" (Morris, 1996, p. 301).

A political scientist, Robert Lieberman, says of Carter that Jimmy Carter was actually who he said he was, something that is very rarely found among the political clan (Gerber, 2023). He is rightly termed as one of the greatest ex-presidents that the US can boast of.

We can only hope that Carter continues to celebrate the last moments he is granted here on Earth. He has nothing more to prove or show anybody. His cup of life has been full to the brim and his maker can have no quarrel with him that he did not strive to live his best life every day.

Conclusion:

99 And Counting

I have one life and one chance to make it count for something... My faith demands that I do whatever I can, wherever I am, whenever I can, for as long as I can with whatever I have to try to make a difference. –Jimmy Carter

In a 1976 presidential campaign, Jimmy Carter was asked what he wanted to be remembered for. His answer gives us a clue as to why the man is relentless in fighting for social justice, peace, and health.

I would like to have my frequent prayer answered that God let my life be meaningful in the enhancement of His kingdom and that my life might be meaningful in the enhancement of the lives of my fellow human beings. That I might help translate the natural love that exists in the world and do simple justice through government. I believe that the almost accidental choice of politics as part of my life's career will have been a very gratifying part of realizing that prayer. I've never asked God to let me win an election or to let me have success in politics. I've just said, 'Lord, let my action be meaningful to You and let my life that You've given me not be wasted. Let it be of benefit to Your kingdom and to my fellow human beings.' If I had that prayer answered, I think I would be very gratified. (Ariail & Heckler-Feltz, 1996, p. 159)

At the time, people may have wondered whether it was only election rhetoric that made Carter answer the way he did. And yet, today, 43 years after the end of his presidential tenure, we know that Carter has been only more eager to serve people around him than ever, even after he no longer had any political ambitions. If health had permitted, perhaps he would still be out there repairing a shelter, saving people from a deadly disease, or brokering peace negotiations in some remote corner of the world.

In another interview the same year, he was asked why he thought we were on Earth and his response was religious but also practically wise:

I could quote the biblical references to creation, that God created us in His own image, hoping that we'd be perfect, and we turned out to be not perfect but very sinful. And then, when Christ was asked what are the two great commandments from God which should direct our lives, He said, 'To love God with all your heart and soul and mind . . . and love your neighbor as yourself'...So, I try to take that condensation of Christian theology and let it be something through which I search for a meaningful existence. But the truth is, I don't worry about it too much anymore. I used to when I was a college sophomore, and we used to debate for hours and hours about why we're here, who made us, where shall we go, what is our purpose. But I don't feel frustrated about it. You know, I'm not afraid to see my life ended. I feel like every day is meaningful. I don't have any fear at all of death. I feel I'm doing the best I can, and if I get elected president, I'll have a chance to magnify my own influence, maybe in a meaningful way. (Ariail & Heckler-Feltz, 1996, p. 161)

In his Sunday classes, Carter was often heard telling anyone willing to listen that the length of their lives wasn't as important as knowing that they had lived it via their God. Carter, who can boast of a long life, can equally boast of a life well spent.

If we are to sum up all the achievements of Jimmy Carter, then probably we can also understand that for him, his morality came before public opinion. He did what was right even when things were difficult. He was honest, and it may have cost him a political position, but it surely earned him an irreplaceable place in people's hearts. America can be truly proud of having placed its trust in him, even if it was only for a single term. His defeat in the next elections was perhaps not such a bad thing in retrospect. We got a man who was determined to fight for causes that no one else had the courage or energy to take on. Carter has indeed done his best for people all over the world. We can only hope now that his actions will inspire more like him to come forward and take on the mantle of responsibility and continue the good fight.

I hope that *Jimmy Carter: 99 Remarkable Tales From 99 Extraordinary Years* has been as interesting for you as it was for me to pen. The research I undertook on Jimmy Carter has definitely restored my faith in humanity and the power of goodness to overcome all the trials and tribulations that one may face in life. Lastly, I would be deeply grateful if you could take the time to leave me a review on Amazon, letting me know how you enjoyed the book and if you were as inspired by Carter's life as I was.

About the Author

Anthony Dobbs is an inspiring biographer and historian with a passion for unraveling the lives of remarkable individuals. With work dedicated to chronicling the journeys of notable figures, Anthony has earned a reputation for digging deep into the rich tapestry of history and revealing the human stories that lie within.

In *Jimmy Carter: 99 Remarkable Tales From 99 Extraordinary Years*, Anthony brings his unparalleled storytelling prowess to the life and times of one of America's most iconic statesmen. With meticulous research and an infallible eye for detail, he presents an intimate portrait of Jimmy Carter, the 39th President of the United States. His writing not only delves into the political and public aspects of President Carter's life but also explores the personal moments that have shaped his character and legacy. From his humble beginnings in Plains, Georgia, to his time in the White House and his tireless work in diplomacy and humanitarian efforts, Anthony paints a vivid and comprehensive picture of this extraordinary man in 99 wonderfully told narratives. With a career spanning nearly a century, Jimmy Carter's life has been a testament to the power of dedication, empathy, and service. Anthony skillfully weaves together the threads of President Carter's experiences, offering readers a glimpse into the wisdom, resilience, and unwavering commitment that has defined his remarkable journey. In this deeply moving and informative book, Anthony invites readers to embark on a captivating journey through history, celebrating the life and legacy of a statesman, humanitarian, and Nobel laureate.

References

Acker, K. (2003). *Jimmy Carter*. Chelsea House Publishers. Internet Archive. https://archive.org/details/jimmycarter0000acke/page/5/mode/1up

Ariail, D., & Heckler-Feltz, C. (1996). *The carpenter's apprentice: The spiritual biography of Jimmy Carter*. Internet Archive. https://archive.org/details/carpentersappren00aria/page/9/mode/1up?view=theater

Beaubien, J. & Whitehead, S. (2023, February 23). *Jimmy Carter took on the awful Guinea worm when no one else would—and he triumphed*. NPR. https://www.npr.org/sections/goatsandsoda/2023/02/23/1158358366/jimmy-carter-took-on-the-awful-guinea-worm-when-no-one-else-would-and-he-triumph#:~:text=%22I%20would%20like%20to%20see

Bird, K. (2023, March 29). *Unheralded environmentalist: Jimmy Carter's green legacy*. Yale Environment360. https://e360.yale.edu/features/jimmy-carter-environmental-legacy

Burack, E. (2023, February 21). *Jimmy Carter's life in photos*. Town & Country. https://www.townandcountrymag.com/society/politics/g41444877/president-jimmy-carter-photos/

Cadwalladr, C. (2011, September 10). Jimmy Carter: "We never dropped a bomb. We never fired a bullet. We never went to war." The Observer. https://www.theguardian.com/world/2011/sep/11/president-jimmy-carter-interview

Capps, K. (2023, February 23). Jimmy Carter, home builder. *Bloomberg.* https://www.bloomberg.com/news/articles/2023-02-23/jimmy-carter-the-president-who-built-houses

Carter and Ford discuss future without Sadat, with Qaddafi. (1981, October 12). *Washington Post.* https://www.washingtonpost.com/archive/politics/1981/10/12/carter-and-ford-discuss-future-without-sadat-with-qaddafi/ab6608ff-5467-4ac5-a5e8-44ef9abdad34/

Carter, J. (1982). *Keeping faith: memoirs of a president.* Bantam Books. Internet Archive. https://archive.org/details/keepingfaith0000unse/mode/1up

Carter, J. (2001). *An hour before daylight: memories of a rural boyhood.* Simon & Schuster. Internet Archive. https://archive.org/details/hourbeforedaylig0000cart/page/n2/mode/1up

Carter, J. (2010). *White House diary.* Farrar, Straus and Giroux. Internet Archive. https://archive.org/details/whitehousediary00jimm

Carter, J. (2016). *A full life: Reflections at ninety.* Simon & Schuster. https://static1.squarespace.com/static/5748890fe707eb4fe6944668/t/5939b197e4fcb561431a796c/1496953261831/Jimmy+Carter+-+A+Full+Life.pdf

CBS News. (2023a, February 21). Jimmy Carter's pastor discusses former president's legacy, faith and lifetime of service. *CBS News.* https://www.cbsnews.com/video/jimmy-carters-pastor-discusses-former-presidents-legacy-faith-and-lifetime-of-service/

CBS News. (2023b, February 22). Jimmy Carter celebrated at trading post in Plains, Georgia. *CBS News.* https://www.cbsnews.com/video/jimmy-carter-celebrated-at-trading-post-in-plains-georgia/

Gerber, E. (2023, March 15). *The best Jimmy Carter books recommended by Robert Lieberman*. Five Books. https://fivebooks.com/best-books/the-best-jimmy-carter-books-robert-lieberman/

Gherman, B. (2004). *Jimmy Carter*. Lerner Publications Co. Internet Archive. https://archive.org/details/jimmycarter0000gher/page/58/mode/2up

gordonskene. (2019, March 26). *Anastasio Somoza—meet the press—1967—past daily reference room*. Past Daily. https://pastdaily.com/2019/03/26/anastasio-somoza-meet-the-press-1967-past-daily-reference-room/

Is Jimmy Carter the oldest living US president, still among us? (2023, September 5). Cooperation of Worldwide Broadcast. https://coopwb.in/info/is-jimmy-carter-still-alive/

Isaac, R. (2005, February 7). *Wine talk: Jimmy Carter*. Wine Spectator. https://www.winespectator.com/articles/wine-talk-jimmy-carter-2389

Morris, K. E. (1996). *Jimmy Carter: American moralist*. University of Georgia Press. Internet Archive. https://archive.org/details/jimmycarterameri0000morr_o1b5/page/159/mode/1up?view=theater&q=ruth

Powell, J. (1984). *The other side of the story*. Morrow. Internet Archive. https://archive.org/details/othersideofstory00powe/page/n3/mode/2up

Printed in Great Britain
by Amazon